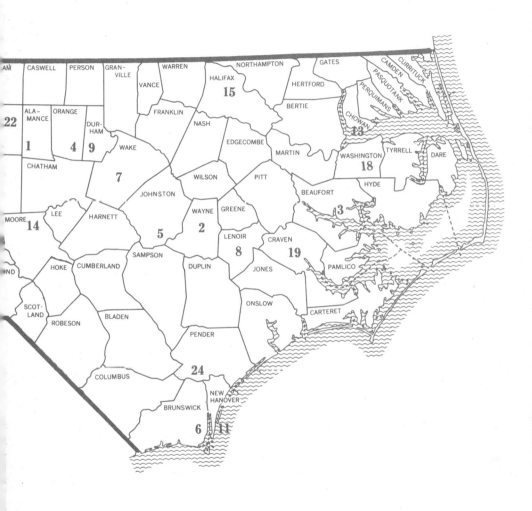

# HISTORY OF NORTH CAROLINA FOR THE YOUTH

# "THE GOODLIEST LAND"

(This name given by Ralph Lane, September 3, 1585, in his letter to M. Richard Hakluyt, Esquire, when he wrote "it is the goodliest and most pleasing soile(land) of the world".)

D0503317

DEDICATED
to
LOVERS OF NORTH CAROLINA HISTORY
by
Ozell Kiser Freeman

Composition, Printing and Binding
The Delmar Companies
Charlotte, North Carolina

Cover design, map, and title sketches
by
William Rankin
Supervisor of Art Education
City Schools
Salisbury, North Carolina




Illustrated
by
Bobby Spires
and
Robbie Watts




Photographs
by
Glenn D. Freeman

*The State Mammal has lunch on the State Tree.*

# ACKNOWLEDGEMENTS

The author has put together this book after much reading and research with the idea of incorporating material of interest to fourth grade children. This book is an informal, intimate narrative of various facets of the history of North Carolina; but, in no sense, is it intended to be all-inclusive, but rather to increase the interest of the reader and to encourage further reading and study of our great State.

I wish to thank the many people who helped to make this North Carolina History possible.

First of all I salute Carl Goerch and the late Bill Sharpe, for "The State" Magazine which through the years in my teaching has provided wonderful source materials of fact and fiction for all areas of North Carolina. I have long been interested in North Carolina history and items from "The State" have enriched it.

In the fall of 1971 Superintendent Harold Isenberg of Salisbury City Schools offered a mini-grant, and when I suggested a North Carolina History for Fourth Grades — the assignment was given to me. Assistant Superintendent Marcus Smith eagerly encouraged me. Mr. Paul Goble, Wiley School Principal, gave many helpful suggestions, proof read, and made plans for printing and binding the first mimeographed edition. Many books and pamphlets were provided by Mr. James Lloyd of the Supplementary Education Center. The Librarian, Mrs. Labe Little, gave me books, films and magazines. Mr. William Rankin, Art Supervisor of Salisbury City Schools, designed the cover, drew a map and made title sketches. Former students, Bobby Spires, High School Senior, and Robbie Watts, Fifth Grade, sketched illustrations. Mrs. Elizabeth Kesler Page, a former pupil of the author, typed the mimeograph sheets for the first edition, and Mrs. Frances Alderman, Secretary, supervised putting it together.

Mr. J. H. Knox, former City Superintendent of Schools, proof read the revised edition and made most valuable suggestions. Mrs. Martha Morehead, Catawba College

English Instructor, read the manuscript and gave me excellent materials. Mrs. Gettys Guille, Director of the Rowan Museum, was a great help to me. Mrs. Cornelia Henderson, Charlotte teacher and principal for many years and author of "Early Charlotte and Mecklenburg County for Children" gave unselfishly of her time and talent to improve my work.

Dr. Cordelia Camp, formerly on the staff of Western Carolina University for 23 years and author of "The Influence of Geography Upon Early North Carolina" reviewed my manuscript and encouraged me to promote this history for the youth. She said, "The book is well organized and gives pertinent facts and interesting episodes. The schools need such material in the elementary grades".

Mr. James W. Brawley, well known author and eminent Rowan Historian, read the manuscript and supplied pertinent facts which were most helpful. Mr. Carl O. Spencer, Jr., specialist in North Carolina Indian lore, gave me interesting facts. Mr. Claude Pickett, well known local historian, revealed interesting facts about Rowan County history. The Salisbury Evening Post has featured many interesting historical stories. I am especially indebted to Mrs. Rose Post of the Salisbury Evening Post who presented my original book in a feature story.

My dear friends, Mr. and Mrs. John L. Henderson, have shown special interest and have inspired me when I would despair. My husband, Glenn D. Freeman, has constantly encouraged me and put up with many a night of "midnight oil" to get the work done. He also provided the photographs for my book.

In my revisions I am much indebted to Mrs. Memory F. Mitchell, Raleigh Editor of "The North Carolina Historical Review" and "Carolina Comments".

Ozell Kiser Freeman

951 Maple Ave.
Salisbury, North Carolina 28144
1977

# CONTENTS

# EARLY MAPS

A good way to learn about North Carolina is to study maps. The early maps show how the land looked hundreds of years ago. One of the first maps published was "Lords Proprietors" map of Carolina, published in London, 1672, to interest the unhappy people in England and Scotland to come to Carolina. Villages were established beginning along the east coast and gradually building to the west along the rivers and sounds. Early maps had five Crane Creeks. One is in Rowan County.

Many of the towns and counties were named for presidents. Washington, North Carolina, was the first town to be named after the President George Washington. Some places were named after local important people. The most honored man using his name for places has been Benjamin Franklin. Can you find the town of Franklin on the North Carolina map?

The highest town in the state is Highlands. Find the elevation and location of this town.

The most southerly town is Calabash. Find it on the map.

FIND THESE UNUSUAL PLACES:

Snake Bite, in Bertie County

Hot House, in Cherokee County

Bug Hill, in Columbus County

Sixpound, in Warren County

Hog Back, in Transylvania County

Whynot . . . Whynot find out for yourself?

HOW DID THESE PLACES GET THEIR NAMES?

Jugtown    Cricket    Wild Cat    Buzzard's Crossroads

HOW MANY NORTH CAROLINA CITIES HAVE BEEN NAMED ALL-AMERICA CITIES?

Consult *The State Magazine* for a lot of answers.

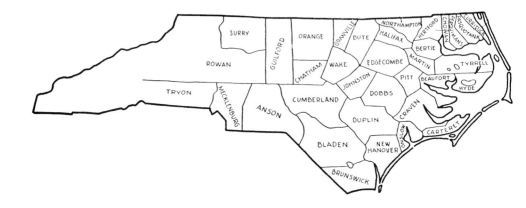

"Showing approximate county divisions in 1775."

The Regions of North Carolina

# SIZE AND CLIMATE OF NORTH CAROLINA

North Carolina is the longest state in the Eastern United States. It is about 500 miles long and about 200 miles wide at the longest and the widest points. In Western North Carolina there are beautiful mountains. Mt. Mitchell is the highest mountain (6684 Ft.) east of the Rocky Mountains. Dr. Elisha Mitchell is buried at the top of the mountain that bears his name. This region is called "The Land of the Sky." In the fall the Great Smoky Mountains and the Blue Ridge Mountains are red and gold. In the spring they are ablaze with azaleas, rhododendron and laurel. The Smoky Mountain National Park is said to be the *most visited* park in America. Grandfather Mountain may be the oldest mountain in the world, perhaps one billion years old!

Below this "Land of the Sky", the rolling hills of the Piedmont Plateau are covered with forests, fields, lakes and rivers. Salisbury is in this region and is 764 feet above sea level.

Someone has said, "The east coast of North Carolina looks as if it were unglued, with long strips of land floating out to sea." This area is called The Outer Banks and is made up of a long peninsula together with Hatteras, Ocracoke, Portsmouth and other islands. At one time this area was completely under the sea. The coastline of North Carolina at one time was near Raleigh. Recently a whale skeleton was dug up in Moore County. The Continental Shelf extends off the coast of North Carolina for a distance of twelve miles. The Gulf Stream is about 12 miles from the tip of Cape Hatteras. The low, swampy region along the coast is called The Coastal Region, or Plains.

Because of North Carolina's location and variations in altitude, the state claims that "You can choose whatever climate you want and find it in North Carolina." The warm Gulf Stream only 12 miles offshore helps to keep the winters mild.

THINGS TO THINK ABOUT:
1. The size of North Carolina.
2. North Carolina's highest mountain.
3. Why North Carolina has such a good climate.
4. Who wrote "The Land of the Sky"?
5. What makes the mountains look blue?

*Western North Carolina Mountains*

# HISTORY OF NORTH CAROLINA INDIANS

North Carolina is very old and people lived here before any history was written. No one knows how these people got here, but some writers think they came from Asia by way of Alaska. When Columbus discovered America in 1492, he thought he had found India so he called the people "INDIANS", and that's what they have been called ever since. Indians were tall and strong and had copper-colored skin and black hair. They were great hunters and trappers, but did not kill for "pleasure" but because they needed the animal's meat to eat and his hide for clothing or shelter. Legend says many Indians thought of animals as "brothers". In those days there were many buffalo and deer roaming the forests. Fish were plentiful in the clear streams and they were used for food and even fertilizer. Besides hunting and fishing, many were "Early Farmers". They raised beans, corn (maize), peas, wheat and tobacco. The squaws did most of the work while the braves hunted and fished. They lived in villages. The houses were made of poles covered with skins or bark. These Indians left no written records but their graves reveal much. When an Indian was buried often his bow and arrows, stone tools, tomahawks, soapstone dishes and the like were buried with him . . . it was thought that he would need them in the HAPPY HUNTING GROUND.

# TOWN CREEK
# INDIAN MOUND

INDIAN MOUND

SPIKES '73

### STATE HISTORIC SITE

Creek Indians migrated here about 1500 A.D. and built their main village. Archeological project and restoration open to the public.

Indian mounds which can be seen today near Mt. Gilead in Montgomery County are most interesting. VISIT THIS AREA.

When the early settlers from Europe came to North Carolina, there were probably 35,000 Indians here. The Tuscarora's seemed to be the most warlike. The Cherokees were the most numerous and the last to be taken over by the white man. Others were the Chowan, the Catawba, the Saponi and the Lumbees. The Saponi lived on the Yadkin River near Salisbury. Two Indians who went to England were Manteo and Wanchese. Carl O. Spencer, Jr., an authority on Indian lore, who thinks that the Indians have made a wonderful contribution to our way of life, says there were never more than one million Indians in the whole United States. He states that there were many tribes and most of them small . . . one that could raise 50 warriors was unusually large.

The disappearance of the John White Colony in 1590 is still a mystery. The drama, "The Lost Colony", is played at Manteo each summer telling about Virginia Dare and the people who disappeared.

The drama, "Unto These Hills", tells the life of the Cherokee.

The Indian, Sequoia, created the alphabet for the Cherokee, making them the most literate of all.

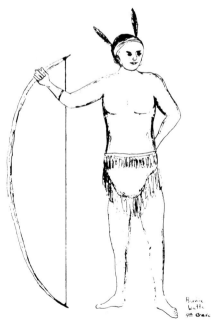

*Early Indian*

THINGS TO DO:

Listen to these records: "Sounds of Cherokee" No. 19028 John G. Burnett's Letter, Erwyn Productions, Box 363, Chapel Hill, N. C.

"Smoky Mt. Ballads", sung by B. Lamar Lunsford with Banjo (FA2040) Folkways Records & Service Corp., N. Y. 36

CROATOAN

Robbie
Watts
4th GRADE

# EARLY SETTLERS

The first Europeans to come to North Carolina were explorers. They did not stay because they were interested only in gold and silver, and not in developing the country.

Then the Spanish came. Almost everyone became sick and died. Later DeSoto came but moved on to the Mississippi River and to the gold and silver mines of Mexico and South America.

Many years later the English came and made permanent colonies. The first colony was at Roanoke Island and was called "Fort Raleigh". On August 18, 1587, a baby girl was born to Eleanor and Ananias Dare. She was named Virginia Dare and was the first child born of English parents in the New World.

Governor White left after Virginia Dare was born and went to England to get many needed supplies. He was gone longer than he expected since England was at war. When Governor White and his men returned to North Carolina he found the little colony had vanished. On a tree the word "CROATOAN" was carved. He searched and searched but the colony was never found.

What do you think happened to Virginia Dare?

*Cherokee Indians*

# LATER YEARS

In 1607 a colony was begun at Jamestown, Virginia. This became the first permanent English Colony in America. This colony faced many hardships. The Colonists quarreled among themselves and had trouble with the Indians. Some became sick and died. Capt. John Smith helped them. The Indians showed them how to grow tobacco. The crop did so well that it turned out to be their biggest money crop.

Dissatisfied and land-hungry Virginia settlers moved toward the Albemarle Sound Area. The first known permanent white settler in North Carolina was Nathaniel Batts. On September 24, 1660, he bought from friendly Indians land **now** 3 miles South of Chowan River Bridge.

In 1629 King Charles I of England granted to Sir Robert Heath all the land from the Atlantic Ocean to the Pacific between 31 and 36 degrees and called it "Carolina". In 1663 Charles II voided the Heath grant and gave "Carolina" to eight "Lords Proprietors". In 1710 they appointed Edward Hyde governor of North Carolina (now separated from South Carolina).

In 1729 North Carolina became a Royal Colony when the King bought back the land from 7 "Lords Proprietors" (except Carteret). The colony became a state in 1789. From 1729 to 1775 North Carolina had five Royal Governors: George Burrington, Gabriel Johnston, Arthur Dobbs, William Tryon and Josiah Martin.

MAKE EXTRA REPORTS:
1. Tryon's Palace
2. Bath (1705 . . . oldest town)
3. Capitals of North Carolina
4. Sketch Tryon's Palace

THINGS TO DO:
1. Read the story of Virginia Dare.
2. See the drama "The Lost Colony."

# MEDICINES AND OLD REMEDIES USED BY EARLY SETTLERS

A hot tea made from mullein leaves was used for a bad cough.

Ground hog oil or a poultice made of onions placed on the chest was good to break up a cold.

To cure poison oak a liquid made from the bark of mountain laurel was rubbed on the itchy spot.

A solution made from oak galls was used to soothe burns. It was the tannic acid that helped.

Sassafras tea was considered to be a good medicine for many illnesses.

Sulphur and molasses were given to the children in the spring to make them healthy.

Snake bite was treated with snake root plant.

The yellow yarrow was a cure for a toothache.

The "Mad Stone" (a gallstone from a deer) was used to draw out the poison when bitten by a mad dog (rabies infected).

# MOST EARLY SETTLERS HAD SUPERSTITIONS AND SIGNS

Tell a dream before breakfast and it will come true.

A whistling girl and a crowing hen will come to some bad end.

Smoke settling to the ground indicated an early rain.

A red sunset was a true sign of a beautiful day to follow.

If a black cat crosses your path, turn your hat backwards or spit in it, to break the spell of bad luck.

Breaking a mirror was seven years of bad luck.

When the family dog "bayed the moon", it was a bad sign, usually meaning death.

When visiting a home, always leave by the door you entered to prevent bad luck.


FOR THE STUDENT:
　　Find other medicines and superstitions of early settlers.
　　Visit the Country Doctor Museum at Bailey, Nash County.
　　Read "Memoirs of a Country Doctor", by Dr. John Robert Lowery of Salisbury, N. C.

READ "A Country Doctor in the South Mountains"
　　by Benjamin Earle Washburn of Rutherfordton, N. C.

# NORTH CAROLINA CITIES

## IMPORTANT COASTAL CITIES
### *BATH*

This is the oldest town in North Carolina and was founded in 1705 and at one time was the seat of State Government. Bath had the first library. St. Thomas Episcopal Church is the oldest standing church in North Carolina and is also one of the oldest churches in the United States.

### *EDENTON*

Edenton served as capital city (1722-1743) under Royal Governors and was named for Governor Eden.

In early history one of the most exciting events here was the famous Edenton Tea Party. On Oct. 25, 1774, fifty-one ladies came to the home of Mrs. Elizabeth King to sign a Resolution vowing not to drink tea imported from England until it was again tax free. At this gathering the ladies drank a brew of dried raspberry or mulberry leaves . . . but not tea. Mrs. King's house is marked by a brass teapot mounted on a Revolutionary cannon.

VISIT the North Carolina Museum of History and see the photograph of the Edenton Tea Party.

Bake some tea cakes and have an Edenton Tea Party.

## RECIPE
### EDENTON TEA PARTY CAKES
Cream together 3/4 cup butter with 2 large cups brown sugar. Add 3 eggs and blend. Stir 1 teaspoon soda into a small amount of hot water. Cool slightly and add to creamed mixture with 1/2 teaspoon salt and enough flour to make a stiff dough. Flavor with vanilla. Chill. Roll out thin, cut with cookie cutters and bake in a hot oven, 400 degrees until done.

From the Tea Party Chapter, DAR, Edenton, N. C.

### *NEW BERN*

This is the second oldest town in North Carolina and was settled by Swiss and German settlers. New Bern was the capital town of some of the Colonial Governors. In 1711 New Bern was almost wiped out by the Tuscarora Indians, but was rebuilt and incorporated in 1723. Tryon Palace built by Governor Tryon was described as "The most beautiful building in Colonial America." This beautiful palace was destroyed by fire in 1795 when a servant went to the basement for eggs. She fell into the hay, dropped her candle, and burnt it down.

Tryon Palace has now been restored and it is a beautiful place to visit.

## NAG'S HEAD

The legend is that Nag's Head acquired its name from the islanders who tied lanterns on the necks of ponies, or nags, and led them across the high sand dunes along the coast. (Some dunes were as high as 135 feet.) The light swinging from the animal's neck would cause the captains of sailing vessels to think it was a light from another ship and cause them to run aground on the shoals where their cargo could be taken by natives acting like pirates.

## KITTY HAWK

Near Nag's Head is Kitty Hawk made famous by the Wright Brothers who made their first airplane flight on December 17, 1903, in a plane with 40 foot wingspan, 21 feet long, powered by a 4 cylinder, 11 horsepower engine, all weighing 745 pounds, which went 10 feet into the air and flew only 120 feet during its 12 second flight.

A fast reader can silently read this account of "Kitty Hawk" in about 12 seconds. Try it.

VISIT KITTY HAWK AND SEE A REPLICA OF THIS PLANE.

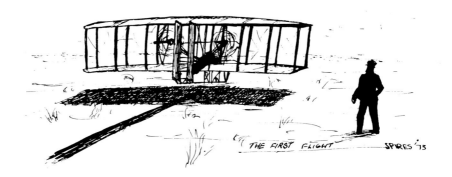

THE FIRST FLIGHT — SPIRES '73

## HALIFAX

In 1723 settlers came to Halifax. The "Halifax Resolves" (April 12, 1776) made North Carolina the first colony to inform its delegates to the Continental Congress to vote for Independence from England. The first State Constitution was ratified here. VISIT THIS HISTORIC TOWN.

## CALABASH

The mere mention of the name "CALABASH" is enough to make one's mouth water for the succulent clams, oysters, shrimp and fish served here daily throughout the year to hundreds of people by a dozen restaurants at this "Seafood Capital" of North Carolina. Try it and you'll like it, too.

Calabash, the most southerly town in North Carolina, was settled about 1880 and was so named because people grew a lot of gourds there.

## OCRACOKE

The Outer Banks of North Carolina are very interesting, especially Ocracoke. The wild pony roundup is something to see. This is the site of the battle where the pirate Blackbeard was killed. The lighthouse is picturesque.

READ the story of "Old Christmas", North Carolina Parade, by Richard Walser.

## FORT RALEIGH

This fort was built on Roanoke Island. It was here that Virginia Dare, the first child born of English parents in the New World, was baptized. The mystery of the "Lost Colony" is dramatized during the summer. The drama was written by Paul Green.

## ELIZABETH CITY

Elizabeth City is in the Albemarle Sound Region. It has been almost 300 years since the first English visitors came to this city. A Christ Episcopal Church is located here. Near Elizabeth City is a hunting ground where wild birds nest during the hunting season. This area is a great place for boating at anytime.

There are other important cities in this section which has been called "The Cradle of North Carolina."

## CAPE HATTERAS

This place is known as "the graveyard of the Atlantic." The tallest lighthouse in the entire country is here. There have been hundreds of ships wrecked on the reefs. Theodosia Burr, daughter of Aaron Burr, may have been shipwrecked and drowned near Cape Hatteras. READ: National Geographic, Vol. 147, No. 1, Jan. 1975, "How we found the Monitor" . . . about 17 miles offshore from Cape Hatteras.

## WILMINGTON

This coastal city, once a Colonial Capital, is located on a peninsula between the Cape Fear River and the Atlantic Ocean. It is the largest seaport in North Carolina. Every year the Azalea Festival is celebrated here. The beautiful Orton Plantation shows a way of colonial living. The U.S.S. North Carolina is a major attraction. In the beautiful Greenfield Garden is a Story-Book Zoo with animals, and rides.

FIND OUT ALL YOU CAN ABOUT OTHER COASTAL CITIES.

*At the Seashore*

# IMPORTANT PIEDMONT CITIES

## *RALEIGH*

Raleigh has been the capital of North Carolina since 1792. It was named for Sir Walter Raleigh. The first capitol building was made of brick and wood and was destroyed by fire in 1831. The roof was being repaired and some burning wood fell inside the building and burned it down. It was rebuilt of granite blocks from a quarry near Raleigh and finished in 1840. This beautiful capitol occupies 6½ acres with many native trees and shrubs. There is a bronze monument in front of the capitol honoring North Carolina's three U. S. presidents: Andrew Jackson, Andrew Johnson and James K. Polk. The new Legislative Building is considered to be one of the most beautiful in the nation. The Executive Mansion, home of the governor, was built of brick and sandstone around 1883 by prison labor.

*Governor's Mansion at Raleigh*

## CHAPEL HILL

The University of North Carolina was opened in 1795. The "Old Well", Old East, Morehead Planetarium, the "Tin Can", and Kenan Stadium make Chapel Hill an interesting place. Memorial Hospital here boasts of some of the best physicians and surgeons anywhere.

*The Old Well at Chapel Hill*

## HILLSBOROUGH (Hillsboro)

Established in 1754, Hillsborough became a hotbed of rebellion against unfair British tax collectors. Several violent protesters were hanged by Gov. Tryon. The North Carolina Provincial Government met here in 1775. Its main business was preparing for war against the British. Someone must have realized that the "pen is mightier than the sword" for in 1777 the first paper mill in North Carolina was established here.

## DURHAM

This city is a leading tobacco center. James B. Duke gave many millions of dollars to make Duke University a great University. Duke Hospital's fame has spread far. Near the city is the Bennett House, historic site where General Johnson surrendered to General Sherman at the end of the Civil War.

READ the stories in N. C. Parade by Walser, "At Lucy Bennett's Farmhouse."

## FAYETTEVILLE

The Old Market House near the center of Fayetteville has been there since 1838 and was a market for about anything the settlers had, including slaves. Civil War battles raged here.

Fayetteville is famous for Ft. Bragg, where so many GI's were drafted for World War II.

Early settlements of Highland Scots at Cross Creek and Cambellton became Fayetteville in 1783. The General Assembly met here in 1789 and chartered the University of North Carolina. In 1795 the first student to register walked 170 miles from Wilmington to Chapel Hill.

## REIDSVILLE

Here is the beautiful Chinqua-Penn Plantation. Plan to visit this interesting place and see treasures from every country in the world displayed in the 27 rooms of the house.

## THOMASVILLE

Located in the downtown business district here is the world's largest Duncan Phyfe Chair. Furniture manufacturing has long been an important industry here.

## HIGH POINT

It was named "High Point" because it was the highest point on the N. C. Railroad (now Southern Railway) when the track was laid in 1855. High Point has the world's largest furniture market and motels are filled for miles around when the market is open. You should see the JC's "World's Largest Bureau", which is their office.

## ASHEBORO

The North Carolina 1,371 acre *first State Zoo* (1975) is south of Asheboro (R-4, Box 73, Tel. 919-625-1250). It's also the *first rural* and *first total natural habitat* zoo. Open year around. YOU MUST SEE IT.

## OLD SALEM

Moravians came from Pennsylvania to North Carolina in 1766. They named their settlement "Salem." These religious people soon started an Easter sunrise service, and it has grown so much that thousands attend this beautiful service annually. The church is on the campus of Salem College. Old Salem is now a most interesting part of Winston-Salem; and if you have not tasted bread baked in their wood-burning ovens you have missed a lot. R. J. Reynolds Tobacco Company is here. Near Winston-Salem is Pilot Mountain, an ancient landmark, and an interesting place to visit.

FIND OUT ABOUT BETHABARA IN 1753.

*Moravian Cemetery at Easter*

## PINEHURST

Pinehurst is the Candle Capital of North Carolina. It is a golfer's paradise. No wonder it has so many meetings and is called the "Convention City"

## BURLINGTON

The city grew around North Carolina Railroad shops. In 1853 the Holt Mill was the first southern mill to make colored plaids. A big Western Electric plant is here.

South of Burlington on Highway 62 is Alamance Battleground. On May 16, 1771, Governor Tryon's troops defeated angry colonists ("Regulators"). The "Regulators" were uprising because of unfair taxes and corrupt officers.

## LEXINGTON

This county seat of Davidson County was created from Rowan County in 1822. Settlers were mainly Pennsylvania Germans and Scotch-Irish. Textile, furniture and PPG industries thrive here.

## GREENSBORO

The city was named for General Nathaniel Greene, a Revolutionary War hero. She had the first steam operated textile mill in the state in 1830. Greensboro is well known as a leader in education. Before 1776 she had the Presbyterian "Log College" Academy. In 1892 Woman's College was founded, which has now become a Division of the Consolidated University of North Carolina. In 1902 she had the first Carnegie Library in the state. A&T and Greensboro College are here. In 1967 Greensboro was named an All American City.

## CONCORD

In 1799 a 17 pound gold nugget was found near Concord and was used as a door stop before it was known to be gold. In 1803 a 28 pound nugget was found. A museum is now being planned at Reed's Gold Mine where gold was first discovered. Concord has since become a big textile center. Cook's Buffalo Ranch south of the city on Highway 49 is very interesting . . . especially for young cowboys.

## CHARLOTTE

This city was called the "Queen City" and was named for Queen Charlotte. In 1780 Charlotte Town was a little village with two streets: Trade and Tryon. Today Charlotte is North Carolina's largest city, and has a major airport. The Coliseum and Ovens Auditorium attract thousands of people.

Carowinds recreational park lies a few miles south of Charlotte and offers "Disneyland" type entertainment.

DO YOU KNOW TO WHOM QUEEN CHARLOTTE WAS MARRIED?

VISIT THE MINT MUSEUM HERE.

## SALISBURY

Salisbury was named after the Cathedral town of Salisbury, England, and in 1953 when we celebrated our 200th anniversary an English representative came with a key to their city. President Dwight David Eisenhower honored us by coming to our 200th birthday party. Daniel Boone lived nearby on the Yadkin River. When George Washington visited here in 1791 a ball was given in his honor. President James Knox Polk's grandparents, James Knox and Jean Knox, lived in the county near Cleveland. Andrew Jackson studied law under Spruce McCay, a prominent lawyer and law teacher of the Colonial Period. At one time Thomas Edison visited Salisbury and Rowan County. Salisbury is the site of the Federal Cemetery where so many Union soldiers are buried. The Historical Society has been formed to save and restore many of the beautiful old homes and has opened to the public the beautiful Hall home which it has purchased. The Community Building has been restored. Salisbury was All America City in 1962.

When was Salisbury founded?

What is the altitude of Salisbury?

What is the annual rainfall?

READ the story of "Betsy Brandon", N. C. Parade, by Richard Walser.

*Salisbury Bicentennial . . . 1953*

## KANNAPOLIS

The largest towel factory in the world is here. In 1907 James W. Cannon, father of Charles A. Cannon who followed, bought 600 acres. He had founded a factory in Concord in 1887. There are now 18 plants with average sales of just under a **million dollars a day.** There are over 21,000 employees under Harold Hornaday who make towels, sheets, pillow cases, spreads and other textile products. Kannapolis with about 34,000 people is the largest unincorporated city in the world.

THE NEW "VISITOR CENTER" DOWNTOWN IS INVITING, INTERESTING, AND OPEN.

## McADENVILLE

This Pharr family textile village just off I-85 near Lowell is now famous as "The Christmas Town". As the Christmas season draws near almost every home decorates a tree or a door with tinsel and lights. Bill Pharr's big Christmas Tree has over 1,000 lights on it. The lake is bordered with twinkling lights in trees that reflect their Christmas Cheer to thousands of motorists who come to enjoy this "splendiferous" spectacle. It's worth driving 100 miles to see!

## BELMONT

This site of Sacred Heart College and Belmont Abbey has grown from a Catholic cultural center into a vigorous industrial community with over 25 factories.

## GASTONIA

In 1964 Gastonia was described as one of the top eleven cities in the nation. Textiles predominate here. Visit the Schiele Museum of Natural History at Gastonia.

## MONROE

The city of Monroe was named for President Monroe. Waxhaw, early home of Andrew Jackson, is nearby in Union County.

34

# KINGS MOUNTAIN

Settlers of German and Scotch descent, who were very religious and industrious, came here and the town was incorporated in 1874. Mauney brothers established the Kings Mountain Manufacturing Company. In 1920 D. C. Mauney and Larkin A. Kiser, father of the author, built the Sadie Cotton Mill. Foote Minerals Company came to develop the rich deposits of mica, lithium and spodumene. The Southern Railway line through the center of the business district helped the town to develop. The Battle of Kings Mountain, October 7, 1780, has made it a famous historical place.

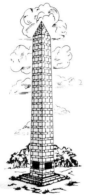

Monument at site of the surrender of the British Forces erected in 1909 by the United States in Kings Mountain National Military Park.

# LINCOLNTON

Lincolnton is a thriving textile town and has the distinction of having had the first cotton mill before 1816. This mill was water-powered but no longer stands. Former Congressman Charles R. Jonas lives here.

SCHENCK-WARLICK MILL

FIRST COTTON MILL IN THE STATE OF NORTH CAROLINA. BUILT BEFORE 1816. SITE 1/2 MILE N.

## HICKORY

In the old days Hickory was a trading center for mountain folk who came in wagons with apples, cabbage, potatoes and chestnuts, feathers, cheese and animal hides. Modern Hickory produces textiles and furniture. Lenoir-Rhyne College lends culture as does the Art Museum here.

## SHELBY

Shelby is a thriving textile town made famous by Clyde R. Hoey, North Carolina Governor and United States Senator, and O. Max Gardner, Governor and philanthropist who founded Gardner-Webb College at Boiling Springs.

The Cleveland County Fair has always been a big attraction in the fall for the entire area.

## WHAT OTHER IMPORTANT PIEDMONT CITIES CAN YOU TELL ABOUT?

## IMPORTANT MOUNTAIN CITIES

### ASHEVILLE

Asheville is a famous mountain resort city and is known as "The Land of the Sky". The well known writer Thomas Wolfe lived here. In his novel, "Look Homeward Angel", he refers to Asheville as "Altamont". He calls the boarding house that was his home, "Dixieland".

### BILTMORE

The Biltmore House, built between 1890 and 1895, is the finest French Castle in the United States. Mr. George Vanderbilt brought from Europe a large collection of art, furniture, dishes, rugs and other valuable things. The estate is over 125,000 acres of forests, gardens, greenhouses and a dairy. The castle built on the "Loveliest Spot in America" has 365 rooms.

## CHEROKEE

This is where Kermit Hunter's outdoor drama, "Unto These Hills", is presented every summer. Here we can see what the life of the Cherokees was like over 250 years ago. The Reservation is located on highways 441 and 19 in western North Carolina. This Reservation is the largest in the eastern United States, and is the home of the Eastern Cherokee.

WHAT name do we give this reservation?

READ the story, "Cherokee Hero", page 88, North Carolina Parade, by Richard Walser.

## BOONE

This is Daniel Boone's country. "Horn in the West" is the drama to see here. Tweetsie Railroad between Blowing Rock and Boone features a steam locomotive and Indian attacks.

Boone is the home of Governor James E. Holshouser, Jr.

Appalachian State University is located here.

Beach Mountain and other ski resorts are nearby. Also "The Land of the Wizard of Oz" is here.

HOW many of these interesting places have you visited?

Which city do you find the most interesting?

How many counties are there in North Carolina?

Make a study of your county.

READ the story of "Tweetsie" by Elizabeth Black.

## VALDESE

Valdese was settled by Waldensians in 1893 when 50 families arrived from the Cottian Alps of Northern Italy.

The summer drama, "From This Day Forward" shows you history hard to believe. By all means see this play.

The Waldensians raise delicious grapes and make fine bread. Nearby is the Drexel Furniture plant.

## LENOIR

The city was named for Gen. William Lenoir of the Revolutionary War. Broyhill Furniture Mart and factory are located here. John Forlines, Jr., is President of The Bank of Granite with main office in Granite Falls.

## BLOWING ROCK

The rock gave the town its name. Ripley called the Rock the "place where it snows upside down". The "Rock" is the most photographed object in the south. The thing here is to be rich enough to afford a home "with a view" of the majestic mountains which are some of the most beautiful in the entire world.

## RUTHERFORDTON

Situated atop a steep hill in the hill country is this sleepy little town in the isothermal belt. Glenn D. Freeman, husband of the author, was born in Rutherford County.

From 1831 to 1857 the Bechtler Mint minted over 3½ million dollars in gold, and North Carolina mined over $50,000,000 in gold. Only California surpassed North Carolina in gold mining after the gold rush of 1849.

## MARION

Marion was founded in 1843. The first court house was the "Carson House", now a museum open to the public. Marion is a busy textile, furniture and hosiery center.

"The Mystery Flower of the Mountains", SHORTIA, was discovered near here by André Michaux in 1788. He carried it to France. No one could find another plant for nearly 100 years. George Hyams went fishing in 1877 in the Catawba River and rediscovered Shortia. The plant became famous and one plant sold for $50.00.

## CHIMNEY ROCK

Chimney Rock is one of the most picturesque cliff-like mountain areas east of the Rockies. The 300 ft. chimney jutting out from the bald faced mountain is a tourist attraction which can be reached by auto. As a youngster my husband climbed the "needle's eye", and the Appian Way to the falls, entered Bat Cave on his stomach, and swam in the swirling waters of the Broad River that cascaded down the rocks. The Freeman House along with the Esmeralda Inn played hosts to celebrities far and wide. On one camping trip Juan Fusté of Cuba, who was just learning to speak English at Westminster School, went to the mountain top and got lost. He spent the night with a farmer and reported next day to worried school masters that he drank "goat milk . . . good."

Rumbling Cave, high on the bald faced mountain opposite Chimney Rock, was so large and had such a high cathedral like ceiling that an entire house could be swallowed up by it.

In later years Lake Lure attracted boating and fishing fans and the Inn catered to famous people.

Earlier history, dating back to the Cherokees, hands down the legend of the ghosts of "The Little People" . . . a spirit world of little people, young and old, that pervaded the Hickory Nut Gorge area. It has been said that ghosts of these little people have from time to time been seen hovering near the Chimney Rock by a number of people. Did the Cherokees see these ghosts, too? In 1966 an old gentleman who supposedly had lapses of memory reported that "The Little People" had tried to imprison him and had held him down . . . so numerous were they . . . but that he "fit" them and got away. It is not known whether he ever knew about the legend or not. But is it not strange that the term "little people" keeps cropping up?

## HENDERSONVILLE

The Apple Capital of North Carolina in the "thermal belt".

***Chimney Rock***

## MORGANTON

The home of Senator Sam Ervin, who was presented the "North Carolina" Award for highest public service by Governor Holshouser, was the first town in North Carolina to adopt the city manager form of government. Located here is the School for the Deaf and the Mental Health Center. The court house was built in 1833. Morganton is now a vigorous industrialized community.

## BURNSVILLE

The town of Burnsville was named for Otway Burns of Beaufort who seized British merchant vessels in his "Snap Dragon" in the early 1800's. The Nu-Wray Inn operated by Rush Wray and formerly by his parents is known widely for its delicious food and "Southern Hospitality".

VISIT the Yancey County Country Store here.

## MURPHY

"From Murphy to Manteo" is about 500 miles and Murphy is the most remote county seat. Even the sun rises ½ hour later here than at Cape Hatteras. The courthouse building is marble . . . the only one of its kind in the United States. Nearby is Lake Hiwassee with a dam 307 ft. high, the highest overspill dam in the United States.

FIND OTHER INTERESTING PLACES IN WESTERN CAROLINA.

# NORTH CAROLINA
# DRAMAS PRESENTED IN
# THE SUMMERTIME

"The Lost Colony" was written by Paul Green of Chapel Hill. He was born near Lillington in 1894. He and Thomas Wolfe were freshmen together at the University of North Carolina, Chapel Hill, in 1916. While in Germany Paul Green began to write dramas. He wrote "Common Glory", which is presented in Williamsburg, Virginia. Another one of his plays is "Wilderness Road" which is presented in Berea, Kentucky. His latest play is "Drumbeats Over Georgia" given at Jekyll Island, Georgia.

The music for "The Lost Colony" was written by Lamar Stringfield, a brother of Preston Stringfield.

This drama tells how life was at Roanoke Island when Virginia Dare was a baby. No one knows the fate of this sweet little baby and the people in the colony. When Governor White returned to the island from England where he had gone to get supplies he found the word "CROATOAN" carved on a tree. The disappearance of this colony remains a mystery.

"Unto These Hills" is a true drama about the life of the Cherokee Indians. It begins in 1540 with the coming of De-Soto. Tsali gave his life so a handful of his people might forever live in the land of their birth. The "trail of tears" is the road where 17,000 Cherokee Indians plodded into exile more than a hundred years ago through mountains from North Carolina to Oklahoma, 1200 miles away. This happened just before the Civil War. The journey took six months in 1838-39. More than 4,000 died along the trail and were buried in unmarked graves.

The author of this drama is Kermit Hunter who graduated from University of North Carolina, Chapel Hill. Every summer this drama is presented at Cherokee, North Carolina.

"Horn in the West" is another drama written by Kermit Hunter, and is presented at Boone, North Carolina. This is the story about the people of the late 1700's. The drama tells about men like Daniel Boone, John Sevier, Cornwallis, Ferguson, Atakalla, the chief of the Cherokees, Nancy Ward, an Indian heroine, and many others.

"From This Day Forward" is a thrilling drama at Valdese. It tells of the Waldenses' struggle for religious freedom from 17th to 19th centuries.

"The Sword of Peace" is presented at Snow Camp, south of Burlington. This drama tells the story of the Quaker Friends and history leading to the Battle of Alamance. The time is from 1751 to 1781.

# THE GOVERNMENT OF NORTH CAROLINA

In the early days the Lords Proprietors established a government for the colony but they never visited the colony. Sometimes the local governors were summoned to England to talk with English officials.

Governors Under the Crown from 1731-1775:

George Burrington
Gabriel Johnston
Arthur Dobbs
William Tryon
Josiah Martin

A Legislature was set up. The people were not happy. From time to time there was a change in the government. The capital cities were many. At last the city of Raleigh became the capital city. The new capitol building was finished in 1840. After the Civil War the state government was very weak. A new Constitution was written in 1868. It took time to establish a good government. In the twentieth century North Carolina became a modern state and grew in all phases. Today North Carolina has the most noted and unusual government building . . . the State Legislative Building. This is the only one in this country devoted entirely to the lawmaking branch of government.

Governor Charles B. Aycock was known as the "Educational Governor" (1901-1905) and his last word as he died while making a speech was "EDUCATION". His monument on Capitol Square (Raleigh) carries the following inscriptions:

## AYCOCK'S IDEALS FOR NORTH CAROLINA

I would have all our people to believe in the possibilities
 of North Carolina
in the strength of her men, the purity of her women
And their power to accomplish as much as can be done
 anywhere on Earth by any people.
I would have them to become dissatisfied with small
 things
to be anxious for higher and better things
to yearn after real greatness, to seek after knowledge
to do the right thing in order that they may be what
 they ought.
I would have the strong to bear the burdens of the weak
and to lift up the weak and to make them strong
teaching man everywhere that real strength consists
not in serving ourselves, but in doing for others.

## AYCOCK'S IDEALS FOR PUBLIC SERVICE

"Equal"! That is the word! On that word I plant myself and my party . . . the equal right of every child born on Earth to have the opportunity to burgeon out all there is within him.

No man is so high that the law shall not be enforced against him, and no man is so low that it shall not reach down to him to lift him up if may be and set him on his feet again and bid him Godspeed to better things.

There is but one way to serve the people well and that is to do the right thing, trusting them as they may ever be trusted to approve the things which count for the Betterment of the State.

# THE THREE NORTH CAROLINA PRESIDENTS

OUR
PRESIDENTS

Andrew Jackson was born of Scotch-Irish parents who lived near the North Carolina and South Carolina state line. Both states claim him to be their president. He grew to be a tall, slender man with a quick temper, which got him into trouble many times. Jackson came to study law in Salisbury and boarded at the Taylor house on South Main Street. About this time many people were going to the new state of Tennessee. So Jackson moved to Tennessee to practice law. Later he built a beautiful home near Nashville and called it "The Hermitage." He became a general and fought in the War of 1812 and won fame as a hero of the Battle of New Orleans. In 1828 he was elected President of the United States. Jackson is one of the many American Heroes.

Visit the birthplace of America's seventh president, Andrew Jackson, at Waxhaw, North Carolina. Jackson was baptised in the Old Waxhaw Presbyterian Church. His father, who died three months before Andrew's birth, is buried in the church cemetery.

James K. Polk was born in 1795 in Mecklenburg County and later moved with his parents to Tennessee. When he was a young man he came back to North Carolina to go to college and graduated from the University of North Carolina. He returned to Tennessee to practice law and later became governor of Tennessee. The nomination of James K. Polk was sent to Washington by telegraph. This was the first important use of the new invention. He was elected President of the United States in 1844. During his term of office the United States went to war with Mexico. While Polk was president Texas and Oregon were admitted to the Union. The Polk Memorial is located on highway 521, just outside the Pineville city limits.

Another North Carolinian, Andrew Johnson, became the seventeenth President of the United States after President Lincoln was assassinated in 1865. Johnson was born in Raleigh. He was three years old when his father died. He grew up and became a tailor, and went to Tennessee to open a tailor shop. While he worked, his wife would read to him so he would be better educated. Later he would hire men to read to him as he worked. Andrew Johnson became a successful business man, and decided to enter politics. He was elected Governor of Tennessee, and went to Washington as a congressman from Tennessee. All of our presidents born in North Carolina later moved to Tennessee. "North Carolina borned 'em. Tennessee reared 'em."

CHOOSE ONE OF THESE THREE MEN AND MAKE A REPORT ABOUT HIM.

READ "Runaway Apprentice", North Carolina Parade by Richard Walser.

*President Andrew Johnson's home
in Raleigh, North Carolina*

Another President of World War I, Woodrow Wilson, lived in Wilmington, North Carolina, for awhile and attended Davidson College, at Davidson, North Carolina.

FIND OUT ALL YOU CAN ABOUT WOODROW WILSON.

Josephus Daniels from North Carolina served as Secretary of the Navy during President Wilson's eight years in office.

Walter Hines Page of North Carolina was Ambassador to Great Britain during World War I, while Woodrow Wilson was president.

# THREE SIGNERS OF THE DECLARATION OF INDEPENDENCE FROM NORTH CAROLINA

The Declaration of Independence was voted upon July 2, 1776. Two days later the Declaration was formally adopted. It was not until August 2 — almost a month later — that the parchment containing the Declaration of Independence was ready for signing. Joseph Hewes, William Hooper and John Penn signed for North Carolina. News traveled slowly over very bad roads in those days. It took 20 days for the people of Halifax to get the words of the Declaration.

# THREE SIGNERS OF THE U.S. CONSTITUTION FROM NORTH CAROLINA
## — 1787 —

William Blount, born in Bertie County. Became U.S. Senator from Tenn. First U.S. Senator to be impeached.

Richard Dobbs Spaight, born in New Bern. U.S. Congressman. Died in a duel with John Stanly, a Federalist leader.

Hugh Williamson, born in Pa. Moved to N.C. Army surgeon in Revolution. N.C. Congressman. Scientist.

The first 11 colonies to join the Union elected George Washington President in Nov. 1788. North Carolina did not join until Nov. 21, 1789. Rhode Island, the thirteenth colony, joined in May 1790.

Some of our leading men argued that North Carolina should not be connected to the other 12 states at all but should remain a "nation to herself". One such person was Governor Richard Caswell, the only Governor to serve a second time: 1776-1780 and again 1785-1787.

Senator Sam Ervin, a great constitutional lawyer, said the CONSTITUTION was the "finest creation of the mind of man". He described the Constitution as the greatest and most precious possession of the American People . . . even more important than our armed forces, our lands and factories.

# THE FOUR FREEDOMS OUR FOREFATHERS DIED FOR:

## THE GLORIOUS HISTORY OF OUR PAST IS WORTHLESS IF WE DO NOT PASS ON THE FOUR FREEDOMS:

Your Freedom to Worship as you please.

Your Freedom of Privacy of your home . . . even against government . . . except by due process of law.

Your Freedom to vote secretly for the government of your choice.

Your Freedom to Write or Speak Your Mind even if you criticize your government.

(Adapted from an advertisement of
The Detroit Edison Company)

# A SPECIAL SALUTE TO MOTHERS

In the olden days mothers spun wool to make clothes, made quilts, churned butter and even chopped wood; but modern mothers also do a "thousand and one" things for the comfort and happiness of their loved ones. Most of the great people we honor became successful because of a loving mother who inspired them.

LET YOUR MOTHER KNOW THAT YOU APPRECIATE THE MANY THINGS SHE DOES FOR YOU. AND DON'T FORGET TO SAY, "I LOVE YOU!"

*A loving quilt maker.*

# A FEW OF NORTH CAROLINA'S GREAT MEN

## SAMUEL JOHNSTON

This man was a leader in the forming of a government for the new state of North Carolina. He became a lawyer. At Halifax he was successful in getting many of his ideas written into the Constitution of 1776. He served as governor, judge, and senator of the United States.

## WILLIAM R. DAVIE

He was born in England and spent most of his life as a lawyer in Halifax. He helped write the Constitution of the United States. Perhaps his greatest service was in establishing the University of North Carolina. In 1798 he was appointed by President John Adams as an agent to go to France and arrange a treaty with that country. Davie County bears his name. Davie was also an outstanding military leader in North Carolina during the Revolution.

## JOHN M. MOREHEAD

John M. Morehead was governor and worked for better roads in North Carolina. He was the greatest railroad builder in the history of the state and was first president of the North Carolina Railroad. The railroad ran from Goldsboro to Charlotte. This line is still owned by the state of North Carolina and leased to the Southern Railway. There were connecting lines from Morehead City to Goldsboro and from Salisbury almost to Morganton and later to Asheville. This helped the Piedmont Region very much. Morehead City bears his name.

## CALVIN HENDERSON WILEY

C. H. Wiley was born in Guilford County and educated at the University of North Carolina. He organized our first system of common schools. He was North Carolina's first Superintendent of Education. He worked for better teachers and schoolhouses. By 1860 the school term was extended to about four months. It was not long before North Carolina's school system was the best in the south. Our school in Salisbury is named for Calvin Henderson Wiley. FIND OUT HOW OLD WILEY SCHOOL IS AND WHO WAS THE FIRST PRINCIPAL.

## ZEBULON B. VANCE

Zebulon B. Vance was one of the greatest leaders in our history. He was a famous Civil War Governor. He became one of North Carolina's best United States Senators in Washington, D. C. Later he served as North Carolina's peace time governor (1877-1879). He died in office April 14, 1894, while serving as United States Senator. Vance County bears his name. To honor him is a granite monument 75 feet high in the square in downtown Asheville.

## CHARLES B. AYCOCK

Charles B. Aycock came to be known as North Carolina's "Educational Governor". He was also a lawyer. He was interested in schools and did much to make better schools in North Carolina. Governor Aycock died on April 4, 1912, while giving a speech on Education to the Alabama Education Association.

## DANIEL BOONE

Daniel Boone was born in Pennsylvania and at the age of sixteen he was considered the best hunter. He lived with his parents along the Yadkin River after they came from Pennsylvania. Daniel's father was Judge Squire Boone and one of the first justices in Rowan County. The family was of the Quaker faith in Pennsylvania, but it is recorded that the Boone family founded and built a Baptist Church on the Yadkin River, "Boone's Ford Baptist Church".

In 1769 Daniel Boone went to Kentucky. His famous Wilderness Trail was 300 miles through rough country by the Cumberland Gap into Kentucky. He fought in the French and Indian War. Daniel's oldest son was scalped and killed by Indians.

He loved the outdoors and was an active hunter all his life. It is believed that in his travels he went as far west as the Yellowstone National Park. But he never forgot North Carolina where he spent most of his boyhood days. The last time he was in North Carolina was probably in 1804.

He died in Missouri. In 1880 Kentucky claimed Boone's body and had it removed to Frankfort, Kentucky, where a monument marks his grave. The parents of Daniel Boone are buried at historic Joppa Cemetery, near Mocksville, North Carolina.

WHOM DID DANIEL BOONE MARRY?

DID DANIEL EVER MEET GEORGE WASHINGTON?

*Historical marker near Mocksville*

54

## SAMUEL PRICE CARSON

A few weeks before the North Carolina Legislature convened in Raleigh in 1822, a young man, just turned 24 years of age, rode out of the mountains of western Carolina to become a member of that body, and thus began an exciting career of service to his country for young Samuel Price Carson, of Burke County . . . later McDowell, of which Marion is the county seat.

He served his country with distinction in two sessions of the Legislature, when he was elected to the National Congress for the 19th, 20th, 21st and 22nd sessions, an era of such importance in our history that it has become known as "the age of political giants."

Already a friend of David Crockett, whose wife was from Swannanoa, their friendship became stronger and more meaningful as later events of their lives brought them together in times of tragedy and significant events. Crockett was at Saluda Gap, just over the South Carolina line, when Carson fought a duel with his political rival, Dr. Robert B. Vance, uncle of Governor Zebulon Vance, and he raced his horse to Carson's home to tell the family that Carson was victorious in the duel. Their lives were interwoven again when both were in Texas, carrying out President Andrew Jackson's orders to General Sam Houston "to take Texas for the United States." Crockett was fighting with Travis and Bowie at the Alamo in a bloody battle with the Mexican troops. Carson was a member of the Constitution Convention that framed the Texas Declaration of Independence and was one of its signers, and while serving as the first Secretary of State of the newly-formed Republic of Texas, word came to him that his friend, "Davy" Crockett, had stood to the last, single-handed and fearlessly beating off the enemy, who had killed all of his comrades until finally they took the life of the man who on this eventful day became a world hero for all time.

READ Moffitt Sinclair Henderson's "A Long, Long Day For November", which is about a North Carolina patriot.

# OLD NORTH CAROLINA MONEY

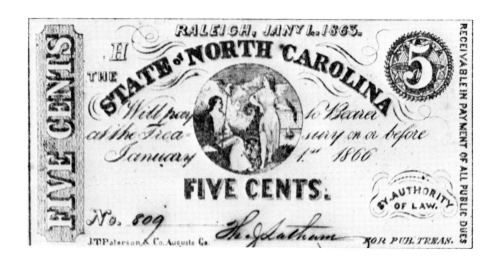

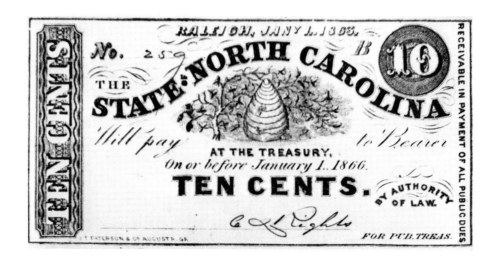

Coins were very scarce in colonial North Carolina. Principal coins were the English Shilling and the Spanish Milled Dollar ("piece of eight"). The first paper money was printed in 1712. In 1780 $725 in paper money was worth only $1.00 in silver. Why was paper money so worthless?

The first bills had pictures of bees, beavers, goats, rattlesnakes, elephants, ships and the Continental Flag printed on them. An English shilling was 12½ cents, the same as a Spanish "bit". (That's why a quarter is "two bits".)

In 1794 corn was given for payment of taxes in Rutherford County. It was valued at 25 cents a bushel. In the early 1900's my husband's Uncle George Freeman gave several days work on county roads in payment of taxes.

The new settlers needed salt to flavor their food and for curing meat and making paper. Salt was hard to get and very valuable. At one time people were given salt as a part of their pay. This was called *salarium* or salt money and from this came our word *salary.*

Fur bearing animals were used to pay taxes. A beaver skin was worth six shillings, deer skin six shillings, and tallow six pence. Salaries for the governor and judges were paid in fox skins. The salary for the sheriff was paid in mink skins. North Carolina printed its last paper money in 1785. Only U.S. money was good afterwards.

The Bechtler Mint began in 1831 and was the first private mint in the nation to coin a gold dollar. North Carolina was the *only* gold producing state from 1804 to 1827. Christopher Bechtler and son, Augustus, came to Rutherfordton from Germany in 1830. They were so skilled in metals that they began to make gold coins in denominations of $1.00, $2.50 and $5.00 and gold jewelry valued in millions near the town of Rutherfordton. At one time their coins were boasted to be more valuable than those made at the United States Mint.

In 1835 a mint was opened in Charlotte. For more than 20 years the mint turned out gold half dollars, quarters and dollars. The coins are identified by a small "c" and are very valuable today. The mint was seized by Confederate forces and was shut down in 1861, having already minted millions in gold coins. The mint was moved to its present location and is known as "The Mint Museum".

VISIT IT.

# AGRICULTURE AND INDUSTRY IN NORTH CAROLINA

When we compare North Carolina with the largest state in the South our state seems small, for Texas is five times as large. Actually North Carolina is small *in size only.*

Let's talk about tobacco first because the white man saw it for the first time in 1492. It was a horrifying sight for Columbus and his men to see dark-skinned natives sending out smoke from their bodies. The Spanish called it "cigarrals", hence the words *cigars* and *cigarettes.* Sir Walter Raleigh introduced tobacco to England. Do you know how much the smoke weighs from a pound of tobacco? Sir Walter Raleigh bet Queen Elizabeth his title against a horse and carriage that he could find the weight of said smoke. Raleigh won the wager and here's how he did it: He smoked a pound of tobacco and then weighed the ashes, which he subtracted from the original pound. The difference was what the smoke weighed.

READ the story of "Tobacco and Buck Duke" from N. C. Parade.

WHAT WILL BE THE FUTURE OF TOBACCO SINCE THE SURGEON GENERAL HAS FOUND THAT SMOKING IS INJURIOUS TO ONE'S HEALTH AND THE GOVERNMENT REQUIRES THIS NOTICE ON ALL CIGARETTE PACKAGES? "WARNING: The Surgeon General has determined that cigarette smoking is dangerous to your health."

In early days of North Carolina the colonists raised cotton and wool to make cloth for their families. There was not much improvement in raising cotton until the cotton gin was invented by Eli Whitney. The gin removed the fibers from the cotton seed. The greatest enemy to cotton is the boll weevil. It damages the cotton boll before the cotton is ready to pick.

There are many things made from cotton other than clothes, sheets, and household articles. Oil from the cotton seed goes into the making of such things as butter, soap, salad oil, paints, rope, paper, medicine, and fertilizer.

*A cotton field in Cleveland County*

The corn raised by the Indians was called maize. Corn was not as popular in the early days as was cotton. Perhaps if more corn had been grown on Roanoke Island, the Lost Colony might have been saved. As you remember Governor White had to go back to England to get more food and supplies. Today in North Carolina a great deal of corn is grown to feed the hogs and cattle.

Lumber and wood products are very important industries. The first paper mill was probably at Salem in September 1789. Today there are large paper plants at Brevard and Canton. If you have been through Canton, you will remember its "smell". Efforts are now being made at better "ecology".

North Carolina has an abundant supply of other crops, fruits, peanuts, potatoes and berries.

North Carolina is the nation's leading manufacturer of fine wood furniture. High Point, Thomasville, Hickory, Lenoir and Morganton are important furniture markets. More recently some makers of molded or extruded plastics (polymers) have entered the furniture field, for instance, Decorative Components, Inc., in Forest City. North Carolina leads the world in textile mills and cigarette factories.

There is a pencil sharpener factory in Statesville. In Sparta the roots of laurel are used to make "briar" pipes. From the red clay of central Carolina Isenhour Brick & Tile and Taylor Clay Products of Salisbury make some of the finest bricks in the world. Pink Granite from Granite Quarry is seen throughout the world in buildings and monuments.

The tourist industry is one of the state's most important sources of income. Our beautiful scenery and parks from the coast to the mountains are known to travelers from throughout the entire United States. The Research Triangle attracts many young people to discover new ideas in science and industry. The many minerals and rare stones in the mountains attract "rock hounds". McDowell County once produced the widest variety of medicinal plants of any state except possibly Wisconsin.

I'll bet you didn't know that early Carolinians raised SILK. In 1731-1755 over 40,000 pounds of raw silk were exported from the Carolinas. The leaves of the white mulberry tree growing here were food for the silkworm. There was a revival of the "silk craze" in 1828-1832 in the Piedmont but it wasn't successful. Today no real silk is produced in North Carolina.

Rice farming was introduced to North Carolina in 1694. Rice was never a major crop like corn and tobacco. In 1753 60,000 bushels of corn were exported to Great Britain. In 1960 the American farmer produced enough food for himself and 25 others . . . in 1974, 52 others plus himself.

*Gina Ross with rice plant.*

*Early farming was done with oxen, horses and mules pulling the plows.*

# A SALUTE TO INDUSTRY IN NORTH CAROLINA

The "climate" of North Carolina is good for industry: plenty of water, temperate climate both winter and summer; good rail, water and highway communication; much electric power; and best of all many good, honest and willing workers who want to stay in beautiful North Carolina with its many parks and playgrounds.

Forty years after the first settlement there were only about 6,000 people in North Carolina . . . mostly farmers.

The manufacture of TAR, PITCH AND TURPENTINE from the pine tree was one of the most important industries until the time of the Civil War.

The Schenck-Warlick Cotton Mill near Lincolnton was the first in North Carolina (1815).

Gold mining was important from 1800 to 1849.

In 1783 to encourage iron making 3,000 acres was given for each foundry built. In 1815 there were 23 foundries. Several were in Lincoln County.

On the Yadkin River in 1898 the first hydro-electric plant was erected. Duke Power (Southern Power) started in 1904.

In 1850 North Carolina had 600 miles of railroads and still had 500 miles of "plank roads". DID YOUR AREA HAVE PLANK ROADS?

In 1860 there were 39 small cotton mills and 7 woolen mills. Ten years later there were 113 cotton mills. In 1973 there were over 8,000 manufacturing plants in North Carolina.

The largest textile research department in the U.S. is at Raleigh. The Research Triangle there and the University Research Park at Charlotte help industry.

NORTH CAROLINA leads the nation in the production of textiles, tobacco, household furniture and brick.

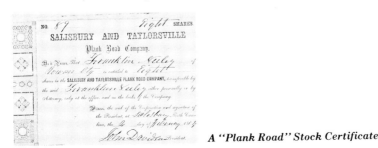

*A "Plank Road" Stock Certificate*

63

# NATURAL RESOURCES

The first Europeans to visit what is now North Carolina, including Lawson, the historian, have recorded their delight in the smiling landscape and the abundance of the wildlife, fruits, flowers and trees. The gentle climate makes for so much beauty in North Carolina.

In the beautiful coastal lands are many beautiful trees. Some are live oaks, magnolias, cypress, long leaf pines and others covered with gray Spanish moss.

The fishing along the coast is excellent. The reason for this is the warm Gulf Stream passing along the Atlantic Coast until it reaches Diamond Shoals off cape Hatteras, the most easterly point of North Carolina. Then it heads northeasterly to warm the western coast of Europe. In this area we find mackerel, haddock, red snapper, striped bass, perch, flounder, blue fish, spots, pompano, whiting, croakers, toad fish and others that would thrill you to catch. Of course, there are oysters, shell fish, muscles and crabs . . . that really take your bait, but gently. There were some whales in the early days, and Carl Spencer wrote about one they dug up near Halifax with its head in one county and its tail in another (maybe)! The porpoise is a native Carolinian and near Lincolnton there is a "Porpoise School".

In the salt creeks of the Carolina low country the turtles are hunted. Alligators still dwell in the marshy coastal region.

North Carolina is certainly a garden land: camellias, japonica, azalea, spirea, wisteria, Cherokee rose, Indian paint brush, iris, tulips, jonquils, black eyed susans, crepe myrtle, all kinds of roses, and even the Venus Fly Trap grows here. Also the rare plant shortia galacitalia which is found in North Carolina and in Japan. And many, many others.

When the early settlers came, the country had quail, herons, swans, geese, cranes, ducks, pelicans, sandpipers, doves, wild turkeys, and oh, so many more!

There are chameleon, red-headed lizard, diamond-back rattler, tiny worm snake, cotton mouth moccasin, brown water snake, copperhead, coral snake, black racer and the spreading adder, which has never been known to bite at all, but makes a big show.

The wildlife in the Piedmont area is different from the coastal region; however, some of the same life will be found in the higher elevations.

Traveling inland from the coast, we enter a broad belt of more elevated, but generally level land. In the hilly country are a variety of broad leafed trees, oaks, hickories, maples, holly, cedars and poplar trees as well as the North Carolina pines.

The flowers are about the same as in the low country except there are more flowering shrubs and trees, such as the dogwoods, lilacs, crepe myrtle, scotch broom and many more.

The fresh water fish are large mouth bass, perch, bream, crappie, catfish and carp. Many of the lakes have fish brought in from fisheries. The walleye is found in the Yadkin River and they are trying to introduce the striped bass.

The squirrels of Carolina range from the mountains to the coast.

We have the mole, red fox, weasel, rabbit, skunk, beaver, otter, 'possum, owl, muskrat, raccoon, and deer living in our Piedmont area of the state. Once buffaloes roamed here.

More true species of birds have been known in Carolina than any other place in the entire United States. Everyone loves the robin, cardinal, blue bird, wren and mockingbird.

The harmless snakes are found all over North Carolina. The snakes found in the Piedmont area are black snake, chicken snake, king snake, ground snake, green snake, copperhead, moccasin and many more. The snake to watch out for in the mountains is the timber back rattlesnake. They are yellowish and blackish with darker crossbands and rattles. All North Carolina snakes that are poi-

sonous (coral, cotton-mouth moccasin, copperhead and rattlesnake) are identified by a triangular head and slanting eyes and a single band of scales on the underside of the tail and are not divided into pairs.

The streams of the mountains are full of rainbow trout, bass and tiny perch. A camping trip is not complete until you go fishing in one of the mountain lakes or rivers.

The mountains are aglow in June with many colors of mountain laurel and rhododendron, black eyed susan and many wild flowers.

Hunters of the mountains see bears, wildcats, deer, fox and other animals. When Daniel Boone hunted in these mountains it is said, "He delighted in the happy hunting grounds and carved with knife, 'D. Boon cilled a bar on tree in the year 1760'". The tree was a beech tree in the edge of Tennessee.

The Great Smoky Mountains to the west are covered with spruce, balsam, white pine and hemlock. Some of the trees are cut for lumber to build homes and furniture. A great deal of these forests is virgin forest where none have been cut before.

### TREES

I think that I shall never see
A poem lovely as a tree,

A tree whose hungry mouth is prest
Against the earth's sweet flowing breast,

A tree that looks at God all day
And lifts her leafy arms to pray,

A tree that may in summer wear
A nest of Robins in her hair,

Upon whose bosom snow has lain,
Who intimately lives with rain.

Poems are made by fools like me,
But only God can make a tree.
Joyce Kilmer

The Joyce Kilmer Forest is near Robbinsville where the last stand of virgin timber remains in Eastern America.

BE A HUNTER WITHOUT A GUN . . . use a camera instead, with field glasses and a note book. Surely lovers of nature are as fully entitled to their share of our wild life as are those who use firearms. Use your opportunities to protect, study and enjoy North Carolina's abundant wild life.

Subscribe to WILDLIFE in North Carolina. Send $2 to Wildlife, Raleigh, N. C. 27611

67

# NORTH CAROLINA GEM STONES

North Carolina stands first among the states in the number of different kinds of minerals. There are 300 different kinds of minerals, but their value is not so great as those of other states. At one time North Carolina was called "The Gold State".

The first gold was discovered in 1799 on the Reed Plantation in Cabarrus County where a 17 pound nugget was found. Not knowing its value the finder used it as a doorstop. From 1825 to 1849 gold mining reached a boom along the Appalachian Mountains and the Piedmont region. Carolina gold was minted into coins at Rutherfordton. Deep shafts were sunk for gold at Gold Hill. Coins were minted in Charlotte from 1837 to 1861. The Mint Museum reminds us of the early mint here, as it was a restoration. Over 5 million dollars worth of gold was coined here.

There have been several diamonds found in McDowell County by small boys. One was found by a young boy going for water to a spring on the farm of Alfred Bright. The lad took it home and it was sent to a gemologist in New York who said it was a fine diamond. A model of it is in the Tiffany Collection.

Paul Goble's great grandfather found the first Hiddenite emerald in Alexander County. He was plowing and found a green rock which was sold for 25¢ and it was worth thousands. This was the beginning of emerald mining and the beginning of the town now known as Hiddenite.

Wayne Anthony of Lincolnton found a 59 carat rough emerald at Rist Mine near Hiddenite and the mine manager paid him $700 for it. This same stone was bought and finished by Tiffany's of New York and is called the "Carolina Emerald" with a value of $100,000.

The finest emerald green colored sapphire in the world also came from Macon County. The hiddenite, or emerald, is only found in North Carolina where it was discovered in 1872. North Carolina leads in the production of feldspar since 1913, which is found in Mitchell and Avery Counties and is used to make porcelain. The light red Rhodolite, named for the Greek word, "Rhoden", meaning *rose* is found in Macon County. North Carolina stands first in the mining of mica in Franklin County. The talc mines are in Swain, Cherokee, and Madison Counties.

In 1767 Josiah Wedgewood, the world's greatest potter, sent an Englishman across the sea to North Carolina to get the white clay from which very fine white china could be made. He had many adventures with the Indians and many hardships in getting the precious clay back to England. After a time the first dishes were made and presented to George III.

Jugtown, North Carolina, now makes a great variety of pottery.

Pink granite is found in Rowan County and has been exported to many parts of the world for statues. Cohen Ludwig of Faith was a talented sculptor.

The granite used to build Ft. Knox where the gold is kept came from Mt. Airy.

Over 90% of the lithium ore deposits of the western hemisphere are in North Carolina. Plants near Kings Mountain and Bessemer City mine this mineral.

LIST the mines in your county.

What buildings in your city are made of native stone?

Make some designs for pottery.

Take a trip to Jugtown. (Near Carthage in Moore County)

READ the story of the "Golden Doorstop", (N. C. Parade . . . Walser)

Visit Museum of North Carolina Minerals . . . Parkway near Spruce Pine

See Minerals Exhibit . . . Museum of Natural History at Raleigh

# NORTH CAROLINA PARTICIPATION IN WARS

There were many attempts for the Europeans to settle in North Carolina. The Indians gave the white man a lot of trouble. It was hard for the settlers to make a living and to have enough food to keep from starving. Later the settlers began planting tobacco and it became so valuable that it grew in the streets. In 1619 Negroes were brought to America to help work tobacco. At the time slavery was also practiced among the various tribes in Africa . . . making slaves of each other.

England was taxing the settlers of North Carolina too much and they began to object. They were willing to pay taxes for goods brought from the West Indies. The first trouble was over the Stamp Act, putting tax stamps on papers, newspapers, pamphlets and the like. They wanted to be represented in their governing bodies . . . the legislatures. So their motto was, "No taxation without representation." However, the Stamp Act was passed. This really made the settlers very dissatisfied. The colonies felt they could protect themselves. Parliament finally removed all taxes except the tax on tea. On December 16, 1773, men dressed as Indians went aboard a "tea ship" and threw all of the boxes of tea into the ocean. It was valued at $1,000.00. This was known as the famous "Boston Tea Party".

The women began to take action in North Carolina. About a year after the Boston Tea Party, on October 25, 1775, the women of Edenton gave up their custom of "tea" until the tax was removed. So this was known as the "Edenton Tea Party" . . . not by a party of "Indians" but by a group of women.

British ships were sent to America, especially to Massachusetts. All the other colonies sympathized with Massachusetts. A meeting was called in Philadelphia and this was called the Continental Congress, since it was a gathering of all the delegates from the North American Colonies. They asked Britain to remove all the oppressive taxes and laws. There was an unfriendly feeling of the colonies for Britain.

On April 19, 1775, a battle between the British troops and the colonists took place at Lexington, Massachusetts. So the Revolutionary War began. (Read about Paul Revere.)

When the fighting began Governor Martin of North Carolina became so frightened that he fled from New Bern, the capital, to a British ship in the Cape Fear River.

On our state flag is a date, May 20, 1775, in honor of the "Mecklenburg Declaration of Independence". The other date on our flag is April 12, 1776, the "Halifax Resolves."

A good many North Carolinians sided with England. These men were called Tories or "King's Men" and fought for England. Settlers who did not think England was fair and who fought against her were called "Whigs".

READ the story, "Mecklenburg Declares Independence", "Early Charlotte and Mecklenburg County", by Cornelia Wearn Henderson.

## BATTLE OF MOORE'S CREEK BRIDGE

The Whigs were at the bridge before the Tories and they had taken some of the planks out of the bridge and greased the logs underneath with tallow and soap so that the Tories would fall into the cold water. It was an awful fight but the Whigs had only two killed and several wounded, while the Tories had around 50 killed or wounded. Guns and equipment and 850 Tories were captured. This was the first battle of the American Revolution in North Carolina and it was fought between Whigs and Tories, all of North Carolina. The promised British help did not arrive in time.

Richard Caswell was the hero and it paid off for him for he was later the first governor of North Carolina. James Moore worked out the scheme that helped to win the battle, but the credit went to Caswell.

Another unsung hero at the Bridge was private John Colwell. The Whigs had fired their rifles and were reloading as the Tories rushed the bridge. The wet fuse of the Whig cannon had repeatedly refused to fire; but as the Tories advanced, Colwell grabbed a red hot stick from the campfire and lit the fuse. The cannon fired with a mighty boom and swept the Tory Highlanders off the bridge to defeat.

## A STORY ABOUT THE BATTLE OF MOORE'S CREEK BRIDGE

## "POLLY" SLOCUMB

Mary Hooks Slocumb ("Polly") spun wool and made her young husband, Ezekiel Slocumb, a special great coat to keep him warm. He loved it so that he took it with him as he marched off with 80 other men from his own farm to join Colonel Richard Caswell's patriot forces to head off the Highland Tories. This was just before the Battle of Moore's Creek Bridge in 1776.

The second night after Ezekiel left, Mary Slocumb had a troubled sleep and awoke after a terrible dream. In the dream she saw a body drenched with blood and wrapped in the great cloak she had woven. She was sure that Ezekiel had been mortally wounded. Quickly she told her maid, "Something dreadful has happened to Ezekiel. Keep the baby. I'm going to find him."

In the dark of the night she raced to the barn and saddled her fastest mare. By daybreak her fast horse had galloped 30 miles. She rode farther and farther. Suddenly she heard cannon shots. She sped on her fleet mare toward the battle at Moore's Creek Bridge. She stopped under some trees, and just like in her dream, there was a bloody soldier lying in a ditch with the great cloak over him. She quickly dismounted and ran to him. She pulled back *Ezekiel's* coat and mopped the blood and dirt from the badly beaten face . . . but it was not Ezekiel! With a sigh of relief, she continued to minister to this wretched soldier. She gave him water. Ezekiel had lent him his coat. Forgetting all else in the midst of a score of bloody men round about, she continued to treat and soothe one after the other, getting water from a nearby stream, washing wounds and binding them with strips torn from her own petticoat.

Ezekiel returned from battle to this scene also bloody and bruised and was startled to see his bride here . . . He asked, "What on earth are you doing here?" She dared not tell him of her dream about the bloody cloak, but she continued rendering first aid far into the night. About midnight she mounted her trusty steed and rode off through the dismal woods, reaching her home and baby the next day, a distance of about 50 miles.

Wouldn't you like to see the statue erected on Moore's Creek Battlefield in Pender County honoring this brave lady?

READ more about Mary Slocum in "Tar Heel Women", by Lou Rogers.

## NORTH CAROLINA INDEPENDENCE AND AFTERWARDS

At Halifax, April 12, 1776, North Carolina declared her independence. So now you know why this date is on the flag.

But as a matter of fact the "Halifax Resolves" notified the Continental Congress that North Carolina was *ready* for independence of the colonies from England, and there was still a lot of fighting to be done.

Many North Carolinians were cold with George Washington at Valley Forge.

When Cornwallis marched into Charlotte on September 20, 1780, he was met from all sides by fighting men from Mecklenburg, Cabarrus, and Rowan Counties. After 16 days he left Charlotte to join other British forces in South Carolina. He called Charlotte the "Hornet's Nest".

Cornwallis sent Major Patrick Ferguson into Western Carolina. The Whig patriots chased Ferguson to the Top of Kings Mountain, where the author as a young girl visited many times. On October 7, 1780, Ferguson was killed and his army wiped out.

The British had failed in North Carolina, so Cornwallis marched into Virginia. But at Yorktown he was cut off from British aid and had to surrender to General Washington. At last America had won her Independence.

**Kings Mountain**

# A STORY ABOUT THE REVOLUTIONARY WAR

## THE DAY THAT SHOCKED THE BRITISH

Little Susan Twitty lived near Kings Mountain and could see where the battle took place and destroyed forever the hope of the British to conquer the colonies. Parson Doaks prayed that the arms of the patriots would be blessed. Her father had told her of the battle. Colonel Ferguson, the leader of the Loyalist army, boasted he would march his men across the mountains, hang their leaders, and lay waste their country with sword and fire, unless they would submit to the king. At last Ferguson on the mountain yelled out, "I am on Kings' Mountain and God Almighty Himself can't drive me from it!" Just then the 900 mountain men were advancing up on all sides of the mountain, to meet 1,104 Loyalist soldiers. John Crockett, father of Davy Crockett, was one of the mountain men going after Ferguson. Ferguson's horse was shot from under him as he tried to escape. He was shot dead with eight rifle balls and his sweetheart died with him there on the mountain. Ferguson's men became so confused (those remaining alive) that they surrendered. The battle began at 3:00 P.M. and was all over at 4:05, Saturday, October 7, 1780. The colonists had 28 killed, 64 wounded, but all of Ferguson's men were either killed, wounded or captured. Ferguson and his sweetheart were buried in the same grave. If you should visit the battlefield, you will find his grave piled with stones. The tradition is to take one and leave another one in its place.

Ferguson and his men did not know that Benjamin Cleveland's command to his rugged, mountain men was, "Go in. Resolve to fight till you win or die, The Sword of the Lord and of Gideon!"

Susan Twitty remembered Parson Doak's prayer had been answered, and the blessing of God upon the arms of the patriots had delivered them at last from all fear of the British. Peace had fallen on the land.

# A STORY FROM THE REVOLUTIONARY WAR

## A FRIEND IN NEED

In January 1781, the British had suffered a defeat at Cowpens, South Carolina. Cornwallis tried to crush General Greene's army. Greene's army was too much for him. After the battle General Greene retreated to Virginia for supplies.

Greene and his army headed for Trading Ford on the Yadkin River and passed through Salisbury. He was tired, hungry, alone, no money and without a friend. Elizabeth Maxwell Steele, a tavern owner, overheard these words of Greene talking to himself, and she felt sorry for him. So she invited Greene to have a hot meal. When Greene started to leave the tavern Mrs. Steele gave him two sacks of gold and silver. This was her life's savings. "Take them", she said, "For you will need them and I can do without them".

It helped Greene to keep his army together and make it into Virginia where he was reinforced. Then they moved back into North Carolina and fought the British at Guilford Court House.

Elizabeth Maxwell Steele showed her true spirit by being so unselfish and helped to make North Carolina great.

*From an oil painting by Evelyn Pence.*

## NORTH CAROLINA'S PARTICIPATION IN THE WAR OF 1812

America and England continued to be unfriendly. The Indians were teaming up with the British. Our ships were searched and they took off the ship all the sailors who were born in England.

In 1812 the United States declared war on England. The war was fought on the seas, in Canada and in the United States. North Carolina sent men to fight, but there was no fighting in North Carolina.

After awhile the two countries decided to stop fighting and neither side won. General Andrew Jackson's victory at New Orleans was fought after the peace treaty had been signed.

READ about the Battle of New Orleans.

FIND some old stories of the Revolutionary and 1812 Wars.

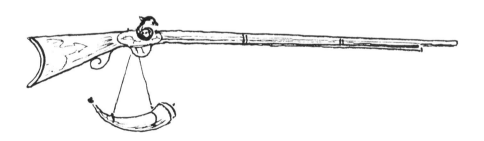

## NORTH CAROLINA'S PARTICIPATION IN THE CIVIL WAR

For years and years North Carolina was not making the progress as many thought she should. The southern states were busy raising cotton and getting very little money for it. The northern states had many factories. As time went on under this situation the North and South became jealous of each other.

President Lincoln took office as President of the United States and in a few weeks South Carolina and other states began to leave the union. The President thought this was not right and he felt it was his duty to try to keep the states together. In order to do this, supplies were sent to Fort Sumter, South Carolina, near Charleston. Of course South Carolina did not like this and the war began. This caused other states to leave the union and North Carolina was next to the last to leave.

During the war North Carolina furnished about one-seventh of the soldiers. Of this number North Carolina lost about 40,000 soldiers. This was the bloodiest war in American history.

President Lincoln was killed by an assassin on April 15, 1865, just six days after General Lee surrendered at Appomatox Courthouse.

Vice President Johnson born in Raleigh, North Carolina, became the seventeenth president.

Under a new Republican legislature North Carolina was admitted back into the Union in 1868 after a long struggle.

CONFEDERATE SOLDIER
1863

SPIRES '73

79

# A STORY ABOUT THE CIVIL WAR

## BEING ON K. P. IN THE CONFEDERATE ARMY

Many a present day G. I. can rattle off good stories about his experiences with KP, but few of them can equal the story told by Grandpa "Bine" Freeman to the author's husband as he sat on his grandad's lap and pulled at his white beard.

Grandpa Freeman and another soldier were not only assigned to KP but they first had to find the food. Their food supplies being low, they had to "live off the land".

They had spied a big turkey gobbler in the yard of a farmer, and the soldiers were extremely hungry. While one engaged the farmer in a spirited conversation facing away from the gobbler, Grandpa eased over near the turkey gobbler and dropped a grain of corn to which a fish hook and line had been fastened. The gobbler swallowed the corn and Grandpa, holding the string, ran as fast as he could to the nearby woods with the flopping gobbler right behind his heels. His accomplice yelled to the farmer, "Bine sure is afraid of gobblers and looks like that one's gonna get him!" And with that he sped after him into the woods.

In the woods that night all the company of famished Confederate soldiers licked their plates clean because the gobbler was so good.

Grandpa Freeman lived to be 96 years old and he always delighted in telling this true story.

*Grandpa Freeman's Kentucky rifle is 5 feet long
and weighs about 10 lbs.*

*Grandpa Bynum ("Bine") Freeman*

Bynum W. Freeman
Pvt. Co. C 10 Bn.
N.C. Hv. Arty.
Confederate States Army
1831-1927

## NORTH CAROLINA'S PARTICIPATION IN
## WORLD WAR I

The first World War began in 1914. President Woodrow Wilson was president. The first year he was president was a happy and successful one. Then some countries in Europe led by Germany and their leader, The Kaiser, began a war on the continent of Europe in 1914. We did not want to enter the war but Germany invaded Belgium, a country that was not fighting. Then, too, Germany used submarines to attack ships. A British ship, the Lusitania, was sunk and more than a thousand people lost their lives. Of this number there were 128 Americans, men, women and children who lost their lives. Germany continued to sink ships and some of them were United States ships. So Congress declared war on Germany, April 16, 1917.

North Carolina played an important part by sending many soldiers to war in Europe. This was the first time that any troops were sent out of the United States to fight in Europe. These troops were from all over the United States. Before the war ended on November 11, 1918, North Carolina had sent more than 86,000 men into the service of their country.

After the war President Wilson worked hard for peace and helped with The League of Nations at Geneva, Switzerland.

READ the Life of Woodrow Wilson


## NORTH CAROLINA'S PARTICIPATION IN
## WORLD WAR II

In 1932 the United States was in the worst depression. People were out of work. There was little money for food and clothing. Franklin D. Roosevelt became president and served three terms and began his fourth term with his popular "New Deal".

The war in Europe began in 1939. The hostile leaders were Hitler, of Germany, Mussolini, of Italy, and Hirohito, of Japan.

On December 7, 1941, the Japanese planes bombed Pearl Harbor, our base in the Hawaiian Islands. We entered the war. The USS North Carolina played an important part in this war. When the end of the war was in sight, President Roosevelt died in Warm Springs, Georgia, on April 12, 1945. Vice President Harry Truman became President.

Dwight D. Eisenhower was a great general in the war. He became President in 1953 when the United States was helping to end another war . . . the Korean War.

The Vietnam War (an undeclared war) was a horrible one in which many North Carolinians gave their lives. Many Americans made it known that they wished to end participation in this futile war, and it was a happy day when the last Vietnam prisoner was brought home by President Nixon.

READ about Franklin D. Roosevelt, Harry S. Truman, and Dwight D. Eisenhower.

READ about Pearl Harbor.

## THE BATTLESHIP USS NORTH CAROLINA

This great ship was built at New York Navy Yard and was launched in 1940 by Governor Hoey's daughter, Isabel, with these words, "In the name of the United States, I christen thee North Carolina." Senator Clyde R. Hoey was a life long friend of the author and her family.

The USS North Carolina is 728 feet long, more than twice the length of a football field, and 108 feet at the beam. Her armor plate was 8 inches thick. In one sea battle a torpedo tore an 80 ft. hole in her but she limped to dry dock for repairs on her own. She could carry 2500 officers and men and four airplanes. The United States government paid $76,885,750 for her. Her 16 inch guns could hit a target 22 miles away. She has been called the "Showboat" of battleships.

Fuel oil for "fill up" was over 2,000,000 gallons.

In 1941 (after Pearl Harbor) the United States declared war on Japan and the USS North Carolina went from the Atlantic Ocean through the Panama Canal to the Pacific. At Pearl Harbor in Hawaii she was to protect the navy aircraft carriers. For three long years she fought in about 50 encounters with Japan with only nine men killed and 44 wounded. She was awarded twelve battle stars. She returned to the United States after the war to be "put in moth balls" because she could not compete with the "nuclear age". She was moved to New Jersey and in 1961 the Navy announced she would be sold for junk. This stirred up many North Carolinians. Leaders aroused interest among citizens and especially school children who together collected $345,000 to buy the USS North Carolina and she was brought to Wilmington. There she is anchored as a "Showboat" Memorial to all North Carolinians who fought and died during World War II.

Guided tours are provided for visitors and people from all parts of the world go there.

READ more about the USS North Carolina.
Be sure to visit her at Wilmington.

*USS North Carolina Battleship*

# SCHOOLS AND UNIVERSITIES OF NORTH CAROLINA

At the beginning of the English Colonies there were no schools.

They had teachers in their own families or they sent their sons back to England to study. In 1766 plans were made to start a school at New Bern. This school had ten poor children who were sent to school with taxes on rum at a penny a gallon.

From that time on schools began to be established in most settlements. The Scotch Irish believed in an education for everyone.

Dr. David Caldwell, a great teacher, had a famous "log college" near Greensboro. The first free school in North Carolina opened in Rockingham County in 1840, called the Williamsburg School. The students studied maps and globes, drawing, painting, music, sewing, and "The Three R's: Reading, 'Riting and 'Rithmetic". Setzer School, now on the campus of Knox Junior High School, was in use in 1842 and is an interesting place to visit and see how an old school looked.

We are all interested in the early schools of our state.

There were some men who took the lead in starting free or public schools. The Legislature passed a law to put some money aside to support schools. At first the schools did not get along very well, and the people decided that one man should give all his time working for the schools of the state. Calvin Henderson Wiley was chosen to do this. No man ever did more for the schools than Dr. Wiley did. There are many schools in the state named for him. Our own school is named for him. He was the first State Superintendent of Public Schools. Dr. Wiley found the schools in a terrible condition. Many of the schoolhouses were small log huts and the teachers were poorly paid. The term of school was only a few months and the attendance was poor. He traveled from the mountains to the ocean in an old fashioned buggy teaching the people about education and getting them interested in schools. Gradually better schools were built. Better teachers were hired, salaries were increased and a longer school term was begun.

Then came the Civil War. Dr. Wiley said the schools must not close. He worked hard to keep them going. The subjects studied up to this time were: reading, writing, arithmetic, spelling, grammar, history and a little geography. During the Civil War the South could not buy the books published in the North. There were a few books printed in the state on poor paper using poor type. Often the teacher was the only one who had a book and she would read each lesson to the students.

One little old book they had was called "First Dixie Reader" by Mrs. Marinda Branson Moore of Raleigh.

Here is a lesson from it —

### "THE CAP"

1. "John has a new cap. His ma made it for him.
2. It is a nice cap, and I hope he will take care of it.
3. Some boys have no ma to make them caps. How glad John should be!
4. Poor Jim Jones has no ma, and his clothes are in rags.
5. His ma died when he was a babe, and the old cook does not know how to fix up boys. Poor Jim Jones."

SEE if you can find some old books in your home for us to read.

Dr. Wiley did succeed in keeping the schools open and we are glad. In 1863 there were more than 50,000 students in public schools. When the south was defeated and the sad days came, the carpet baggers had control, and most of the schools were forced to close for lack of money. The ones that did remain open, Dr. Wiley reported, had glass windows and the buildings had two or three rooms, instead of one. Usually the schoolhouses were built like a square box with a stove heating the schoolroom.

Slowly things began to improve and graded schools were started in Greensboro (1875), in Raleigh (1877) and in Salisbury (1880).

When Governor Jarvis came into office the schools began to show a great improvement. The brightest spot in education came when Charles B. Aycock was elected governor. He believed in free public schools, supported by the taxes of all people, to give to every child in North Carolina a chance to get the best possible education. He worked hard for new buildings and longer school term.

Dr. Charles McIver, the first president of North Carolina College for Women, helped Governor Aycock work for better schools. Also he helped to put into law that every child must attend school. Governor Aycock became known as the "Educational Governor of North Carolina".

The University of North Carolina was chartered in 1793, and buildings were begun and the first students arrived in 1795. Soon afterwards different churches started colleges. The Baptists had Wake Forest; the Presbyterians had Davidson College; the Methodists had Trinity College (later it became Duke University) for boys, and Greensboro College for girls. The Quakers had Guilford College. The Moravians had Salem College for girls. In 1891 Lenoir College was opened in Hickory and later became Lenoir Rhyne College now operated by the Lutheran Church Synod of North Carolina. In 1834 the Reformed Church opened Catawba College at Newton, and was moved to Salisbury in the 1920's. Belmont Abbey was opened by the Catholic Church in 1876. Queen's College was opened in 1771. Today North Carolina has 62 colleges; 41 private schools and 4 theological seminaries, and many technical schools.

Would you believe that the first motor truck for carrying students to school was bought in Pamlico County in 1907?

You should realize more than ever what your state has done for you in making the schools of this state what they are today. Our schools have had the best system in the South since 1860.

# OLD RHYMES AND GAMES

In early schools many "rounds" were sung, such as, "Three Blind Mice", "Row, Row Your Boat", "Scotland's Burning", "The Farmer Takes a Wife", "Old McDonald Had a Farm", etc.

PERHAPS YOU CAN FIND OTHERS TO SING.

Writing in "Memory Books" or "Autograph Books" was very popular. Here are some old ones I found in the "State Magazine", May 11, 1963:

"When you are old and cannot see,
Put on your specks and think of me."

"Remember me, dear friend,
When on these lines you look,
Remember it was I,
Who wrote in your book."

"I know a boy, and I am he,
Who loves a girl, and you am she."

"When rocks and hills divide us
and you I cannot see,
Remember I will be a friend to thee."

"May your life have just 'nough clouds to make a glorious sunset."

"When you stand before the tub,
Think of me before you rub."

At recess time in school many old games were played. The most favored was "Old Fox". Two teams are chosen with a home base for each. Old Fox is chosen and he prowls from one base to the other until a loud chant is given:

"Whatcha gonna do when the Old Fox comes?" All the others shout: "Run Home!" The side that catches the most for his side and can get the players from Old Fox wins the game.

This old counting rhyme was used by a group to select one known as "IT".

"William, William Tremble Toe,
He's a good fisherman,
Catches his hens
Puts them in pens.
Some lay eggs,
Some lay none.
Wire, brier, limber-lock,
Sit and sing till twelve O'clock.
The clock struck one,
The mouse ran down,
O-U-T spells "out",
You dirty old dish rag. . . YOU!" (Pointing to one of the players.) You're IT. IT is sent out of the room, and the other players choose an animal name for themselves, such as dog, bear, horse, etc. IT is given a name also but he does not know what it is. When IT returns to the room, he is asked what he would rather ride home on. If IT guesses his own animal name, he walks home on tip toe. If he names an animal chosen by another player, then that player has to carry IT on his back — piggy back fashion. The "animal" asks his rider, "What have you got there?" "A bag of nits, shake it till it spits!" The "animal" then tries hard to throw his rider off.

CAN YOU FIND OTHER OLD GAMES FOR US TO PLAY?

CREATE A GAME FROM YOUR OWN NAME, Using North Carolina facts, such as:

**F** irst English Settlement was at Roanoke Island.

**R** egulators fought Gov. Tryon's forces at Alamance.

**E** denton Tea Party was held in 1774.

**E** nglish was not the only language spoken by early settlers.

**M** oore's Creek Bridge was the first battle of the Revolution in the state.

**A** ndrew Jackson was born in North Carolina.

**N** orth Carolina is the state I love.

# WEATHER FORECASTING RHYMES
## (The State . . . 2/18/61)

"Evening red and morning gray,
Help the traveler on his way.
Evening gray and morning red,
Bring down rain upon his head."

"A red sun has water in his eye".

"When the clouds do weave,
'Twill storm before they leave."

"In the morning, mountains,
In the evening, fountains."

"When round the moon there is a brugh, (halo),
The weather will be cold and rough."

"Mist on the hills,
Water in the mills"

"Mackerel sky and mare's tails,
Make lofty ships carry low sails."

"The clouds look as if scratched by a hen,
Get ready to reef your topsails then."

"Rainbow in the morning,
Sailors take warning.
Rainbow at night,
Sailor's delight."

"When the hair turns damp in the scalp house,
it will bring rain."

"Drains and swamps smell strongest before a storm."

"Swallows fly low before a rain."

Formula for telling temperature with crickets: Count
cricket chirps for 14 seconds and add 40.

# THE "VERY IMPORTANT" PEOPLE IN NORTH CAROLINA

*. . . NORTH CAROLINA WRITERS . . .*

We have already read about many North Carolinians. The first group is about our state writers. Perhaps one of our most recent writers of note is a Salisbury lady, Mrs. Moffitt Sinclair Henderson (Mrs. John Henderson), who wrote "A Long, Long Day for November", for which she received the Thomas Wolfe Award (1972).

O'Henry (William Sidney Porter) of Greensboro wrote over 250 short stories. He was considered to be the "father" of the American short story.

John Charles McNeill, born at Riverton in Scotland County in 1874, was known as "the state's sweetest singer". In 1905 he was awarded the Patterson Cup by President Theodore Roosevelt for the best poetic writing of the year.

George Moses Horton liked to make up love poems from the time he was 14 years old. He would recite these poems to the students at the University of North Carolina who would often pay him from 25¢ to 75¢ for reciting. Later he was taught how to read and write and he wrote a book in 1829, "The Hope of Liberty". It was the first book written by a Negro in the South.

James Larkin Pearson, North Carolina's only Poet Laureate, celebrated his 96th birthday, Sept. 16, 1976. He wrote "Fifty Acres", "Far Places," "Milkin' Time" and others.

Richard Creecy (Chowan County, 1813) wrote "Grandfather Tales of North Carolina History."

Carl Spencer, famous Spencer historian, knows all there is to know about the Indians of North Carolina and has a fabulous collection of artifacts. YOU SHOULD READ HIS STORIES.

Christian Reid was born in Salisbury in 1846. Her maiden name was Frances Fisher. Her father was the first Confederate Colonel to die in the Civil War at Bull Run. Miss Fisher was married to Mr. Tiernan. She wrote more than 20 novels. Carolinians will remember her for "Land of the Sky". Today her books and mementoes are at the Public Library. There is a stone tablet placed in memory of her on Innes Street. Remember her pen name is Christian Reid.

Thomas Wolfe was born in Asheville. His famous book is "Look Homeward Angel".

Ellis Credle was born in Hyde County in 1902. Some of her stories are: "Down Down the Mountain", "The Blue Ridge Country", "Across the Cotton Patch", "Tall Tales from the Hills", and "Big Fraid, Little Fraid".

Carl Sandburg lived on a farm near Flat Rock. He was not born in North Carolina, but he lived a long time here and wrote many beautiful poems. His books on Lincoln are very famous.

James Shober Brawley, Rowan historian, author of "The Rowan Story", completed a scientific history for the Bicentennial in 1953 and helped to organize the Rowan Museum Corporation.

Many people remember Archibald Henderson as biographer for George Bernard Shaw.

Carl Goerch has probably written more about North Carolina than any living person. "The State Magazine" has been a source of interesting facts about North Carolina. He and the late Bill Sharpe did more to whet my appetite for collecting stories and legends and facts about North Carolina than anybody.

A former Livingstone College Professor, J. Mason Brewer, wrote "Worser Days and Better Times", the Folklore of the North Carolina Negro (Quadrangle Books, Chicago)

Hugh T. Lefler, born in Davie County in 1901 and a Professor of History at the University of North Carolina, has published two great volumes on "North Carolina . . . History, Geography, Government . . ." and others. Every school should have his works in the library.

Jonathan Daniels was born in Raleigh in 1902. He wrote "Tar Heels", "Thomas Wolfe" and many more.

Legette Blythe was born in Huntersville in 1900. He wrote "Marshall Ney: a Dual Life".

Dr. Cordelia Camp, a member of the staff at Western Carolina University for 23 years, wrote "The Influence of Geography Upon Early North Carolina."

Mrs. Cornelia Wearn Henderson, a teacher and principal in Charlotte-Mecklenburg Schools has written "Early Charlotte and Mecklenburg County for Children" and "The Descendants of James Stafford."

Richard Walser was born in Lexington in 1908. His book, "North Carolina Parade", with Julia M. Street is an interesting book about Tar Heels for young people.

John Harden was born in Graham in 1903. He wrote "The Devil's Tramping Ground", "Tar Heel Ghosts", and many other North Carolina mystery stories.

Manly Wade Wellman lives in Chapel Hill. He has written "The Battle of Kings Mountain," "Mystery of Bear Paw Gap", and other tales of North Carolina folklore.

George F. Scheer and Julian Scheer are brothers. Their famous stories are "Rain Makes Applesauce" and "Rebels and Redcoats".

Burke Davis was born in Durham in 1913. He wrote "Robert E. Lee" and "They Called Him Stonewall".

Elizabeth Black of Tryon wrote "Tweetsie", a history of the mountain railroad.

Dr. John Robert Lowery of Salisbury was born in Davie County in 1881 and wrote "Memoirs of a Country Doctor".

Benjamin Earle Washburn of Rutherford County wrote "A Country Doctor in the South Mountains."

MANY OTHER WRITERS CAME TO NORTH CAROLINA TO LIVE. TRY TO FIND OUT WHO THEY WERE.

## NORTH CAROLINA ARTISTS

Our great artist is Elliott Daingerfield of Blowing Rock. His paintings are in the Metropolitan and the Museum of Art in New York, and the National Gallery at Washington, D.C.

Henry Bacon of Wilmington was the Architect of the Lincoln Memorial at Washington, D.C.

Mel Kester of Concord and Bob Timberlake of Lexington have achieved wide acclaim as gifted artists.

Joe King of Winston-Salem painted a portrait of President Nixon for Duke University. His superb painting of Queen Elizabeth hangs in the lobby of the Executive Building in Raleigh.

## NORTH CAROLINA MUSICIANS

Lamar Stringfield started the North Carolina State Symphony in 1932.

Dr. Benjamin Swalin has been the conductor of the symphony for many years. Since his retirement John Gosling is the conductor. The students of the Salisbury City Schools and Rowan County Schools have the opportunity to see and hear the North Carolina State Symphony every year. Do you have this opportunity?

Rob Roy Perry was born in Japan. He came to Hickory and Salisbury where he composed 150 compositions.

Kay Kyser was born at Rocky Mount. He became a Tar Heel musical star. He married Georgia Carroll. For many years they lived at Chapel Hill. Now the "Old Perfesser" of the "Kollege of Musical Knowledge" is in the service of the Christian Science Church and lives in Boston.

Andy Griffith and "Aunt Bee" always "sing" praises to North Carolina and "Raleigh". His TV comedy show has top ratings. Andy was reared in North Carolina.

## NORTH CAROLINA INVENTORS

How many of you knew that the inventor of the "Gatling" gun was a North Carolinian? Richard Jordan Gatling was born in Hertford County in 1818. He invented a rapid firing gun that would fire 200 shots a minute. General Ben Butler bought 12 guns and used them successfully at the seige of Petersburg. The Gatling Gun was officially adopted in 1866, after the Civil War was over.

Carbine Williams invented the Carbine Rifle.

Acetylene gas was invented by Thomas Leopold Wilson of Spray in 1892.

## OTHER FAMOUS NORTH CAROLINA PEOPLE

WHISTLER'S MOTHER, Anna McNeill Whistler, lived near Clarkton on Highway 701 (1804-1881), and was born in Wilmington. Her son, James, painted her portrait in 1871. This painting was bought for $620 and now hangs in the Louvre in Paris, where it is insured for 1½ million dollars.

The great First Lady, Dolley Madison, was born in Guilford County and became the wife of James Madison, the fourth president of the United States.

READ ABOUT THIS GRACIOUS AND BEAUTIFUL LADY.

The two FATHER AND SON governors of North Carolina have been Richard Dobbs Spaight and son, Richard Dobbs Spaight, Jr.; and Kerr Scott and son, Robert Scott.

Actress Ava Gardner is a North Carolina native.

Anne Jeffreys is from Goldsboro.

Sidney Blackmer of Salisbury rose higher and higher on account of his fine appearance and southern voice and became famous in Hollywood and on television.

Annie Oakley lived in North Carolina. Read about her in *State Magazine*, January 1967.

Billy Graham, the world famous evangelist, was born on a farm near Charlotte and now lives in Montreat.

Senator Sam Ervin has retired and lives in Morganton.

The world famous Siamese Twins, Eng and Chang Bunker, became farmers near Mt. Airy and North Wilkesboro. They are buried half way between Mt. Airy and Dobson on old Highway 601.

## THE SIAMESE TWINS WHO "CHOSE" NORTH CAROLINA AS THEIR HOME

At White Plains, N. C., a grave marks the resting place of Chang and Eng Bunker, the original "Siamese Twins", the world famous twin brothers joined together at the breastbone, who lived thus together until death at the age of 63, January 7, 1874. Born in Siam, they were discovered by Robert Hunter, a British merchant; and at the age of 18 they met P. T. Barnum, the greatest American showman, who exhibited the twins throughout the world and made them famous and rich. Surgeons declined to separate the twins lest they die; but they developed great agility and could run, jump and swim together. In later life they became farmers and expert carpenters. One would lay shingles for a roof while the other nailed them. Near North Wilkesboro they met and married two sisters, Sarah and Adelaide Yates, who bore them 22 children. They built two homes about a mile apart and spent 3 nights with one wife and 3 nights with another, and being Baptists they probably rested on the seventh day.

On their world tours with Barnum they became very wealthy and bought a plantation with slaves and livestock in North Carolina. They were very industrious and did well with their farming and other work. They were "smart" because after touring the entire world they "chose" the North Carolina hills as their home. They took to the road several times later to make money for their large families. Chang, often a heavy drinker, suffered ill health and a stroke. Eng was healthier, but when Chang died . . . Eng expired shortly thereafter on the same day. An autopsy after their deaths proved that they could not have survived if the ligament joining them had been severed early in life.

# HISTORIC SITES IN SALISBURY AND ROWAN COUNTY

Two large movements of people came into Salisbury area. The families of Lyerly, Trexler, Brown, Miller and others settled on the east side of Salisbury and helped establish the Lutheran and Reformed Churches. St. John's Lutheran Church was built in 1768, the first one in Salisbury. The families of Graham, Knox and Scotch-Irish people settled west of Salisbury and started the Presbyterian Church.

Here is a list of the well-known people who helped establish Salisbury through the years:

John Mitchell 1771 — Mitchell Avenue
William H. Horah 1842 — Horah Street
John W. Ellis 1855 — Ellis Street
J. H. Innes 1867 — Mayor and Innes Street
Frank B. John 1880 — Elementary School Principal
A. H. Boyden 1881 — Postmaster

## MAXWELL CHAMBERS HOUSE

This house is located on South Jackson Street near the Presbyterian Church. It is over 150 years old. It was bought by Maxwell Chambers about 1850. It is The Rowan Museum today. Take your family to visit this old house.

## PURCELL'S DRUG STORE

This building still stands on the corner of Main and Innes Streets. It was built in 1790-1820 and has been a drug store until 1975. Then it was said to be the tallest building in the state.

## THE LECTURE ROOM OF THE
## PRESBYTERIAN CHURCH

This little house has one room which was used as a Primary Sunday School Room. It is located on the corner of Innes and Jackson Streets. Beneath this building are ten graves, nine of them are covered with marble slabs and one is marked by a headstone. The oldest grave here is marked November 22, 1799. Maxwell Chambers and his family are buried here.

## LAW OFFICE OF ANDREW JACKSON AND
## THE OLD WELL

President Andrew Jackson studied law in Salisbury in a little office near the corner of Fisher and Church Streets. South of the site of this office still stands the original structure of the Old Well.

## THE JAIL

In 1754 a log jail with a log floor was built. It was just one room. The windows had iron rods over them. Some prisoners were punished at the "Whipping Post", or placed in stocks.

**Stocks at Salisbury**

## THE GRAVE OF MARSHALL NEY

West of Salisbury in the graveyard of Old Third Creek Presbyterian Church, is the grave of Marshall Ney. He was Napoleon's "Right Hand" man who was supposed to have been executed, but escaped to America. He is buried under the name Peter Stewart Ney, which he took when he came to America. On the church grounds is a little log schoolhouse, now bricked over where Peter Ney taught school.

## THE FIRST AMERICAN GOLD RUSH

This took place at Gold Hill located 17 miles Southeast of Salisbury on Highway 52. Gold was first known to be in Rowan County in 1799. But not until 1842 when the Gold Hill Company began to operate did it become big business. Many shafts were sunk in the ground about 800 feet. At one time Thomas Edison visited the Gold Hill mine.

## SETZER SCHOOL

The original site of the school is about 11 miles south of Salisbury on the Lentz Road. It was first built in 1842. The school was moved and restored to the grounds of Knox Junior High School in 1962.

There is an old school in Robeson County.

Visit an old one room school near you.

## BOONE'S CAVE

Boone's Cave is where Daniel Boone hid from the Indians. It is located north of Salisbury on the Yadkin River. The parents of Daniel Boone, Sarah and Squire are buried 18 miles north west of Salisbury near Mocksville.

## THE "OLD STONE HOUSE"

This house was built in 1766 of granite bricks, laid in the cement of the day. This is the oldest German home in North Carolina. Michael Braun lived here. The Browns of Rowan County are descendents of Michael Braun. The family graveyard is across the road surrounded by a stone wall. The road between the house and the graveyard was an Indian Trail to Trading Ford on the Yadkin River. The Braun House was purchased by the Rowan Museum in 1959.

OLD STONE HOUSE

## TWO OLD CEMETERIES

The Old Lutheran Cemetery dating back to 1768 is located on North Lee Street. The Old English Cemetery dating from 1775 is located on North Church Street. Some Revolutionary Soldiers both American and English and the body of Governor John W. Ellis are buried there. Why don't you take time to walk through these cemeteries and see if you can find some of your ancestors?

# TWO OLD CHURCHES

About ten miles southeast of Salisbury stands the original structure of Organ (Lutheran) Church built in 1791. Organ Church was organized in 1745.

The Lower Stone (Reformed) Church is about the same distance from Salisbury. The present church was built about 1824.

*On August 12, 1973, the Bicentennial of Lutheranism in America was celebrated at Organ Church and a monument to Pastor Nussmann and Teacher Arends was unveiled.*

## THYATIRA

Thyatira Presbyterian Church, "The Westminister Abbey of Rowan", is located about twelve miles southwest of Salisbury. This Church was established on January 18, 1753. The church there now was built in 1860. Back of this church is the cemetery where some of the most famous North Carolinians of that period are buried. John Knox and Jean Knox, the grandparents of President James K. Polk, and Vice President Alben Barkley's ancestors are buried there.

# SOME OF NORTH CAROLINA'S HISTORICAL SITES

Tryon Palace at New Bern was constructed 1767-1770.

Old Salem at Winston Salem has many old restored houses and buildings showing the life of the 1700's when the Moravians came to North Carolina.

St. Thomas Church at Bath built in 1734-1740 is the oldest church and is still being used. The old Bible in the church is dated 1703. The tile floor of the church covers the graves of many early settlers. Bath is North Carolina's oldest town (1705).

The State Capitol in Raleigh is one of the most beautiful public buildings in the nation.

The Governor's Mansion is of Victorian style of the 1800's and looks like a big "Gingerbread House".

North Carolina Museum of Art was opened in 1956, and is located off Capitol Square in Raleigh. The Museum collections consist of over 1,000 works of art valued at about seven and a half million dollars. There are paintings by Rembrandt, Goya, Stuart, Gainsborough, Reynolds, and many other famous painters.

## VISIT THIS MUSEUM

The site of President Andrew Johnson's birthplace is in Raleigh.

President James K. Polk, the eleventh President of the United States, was born in 1795. The two story reconstructed house near Pineville can be visited, but it is not the original home.

Carl Sandburg's house is at Flat Rock. It is a national shrine.

One should not miss seeing the Biltmore House near Asheville. It has 365 rooms.

It is not far from Salisbury to Reidsville to visit the beautiful Chinqua-Penn Plantation House and gardens.

*Biltmore House at Asheville*

*State House at Raleigh*

*State Capitol at Raleigh*

# NORTH CAROLINA LEGENDS

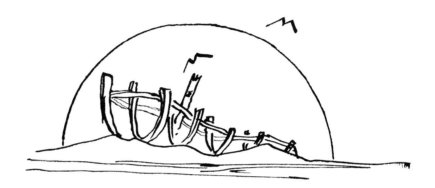

## *CARROL A'DEERING, GHOST SHIP OF THE DIAMOND SHOALS*

Off the coast of Cape Hatteras on the morning of January 31, 1921, the five mast schooner, Carrol A'Deering, was sighted aground. When the lifesavers from the Coast Guard Station reached the schooner they found charts scattered around the captain's room and food set out on the stove, but no sign of the crew. It's still a mystery as it was on that cold morning in January 1921.

Some think there was mutiny on board. Others believe pirates came on board and murdered all the crew. Perhaps a storm caused the crew to leave the ship and sail away in life boats.

It is still a riddle to know that the ship had all sails set, food on the stove and tables and yet no one on board.

## THE PATRIOT

North Carolina coast has been called the "Graveyard of the Atlantic". One of the ships wrecked was the Patriot. In February, 1812, the Patriot left Georgetown, South Carolina, going to New York. One of the passengers was Theodosia Burr Alston, wife of the Governor of South Carolina, and the daughter of the former Vice President of the United States, Aaron Burr. The ship never reached New York, and after much searching it was decided that the ship must have been lost at sea. Many years later a doctor in Elizabeth City was given a portrait in payment for some work he had done for a poor old woman. She told him this story:

"A boat drifted ashore at Nag's Head with no one on board. The boat was examined and the woman's portrait was found. My sweetheart gave it to me."

Years later the Burr family realized how much it looked like Theodosia. As time passed two criminals admitted they were members of a pirate ship who went aboard the Patriot and forced all the passengers off. A dying beggar confessed he was one of the pirates and that he had been haunted by the beautiful woman who had pleaded for her life that she might go to her father in New York.

Was she Theodosia Burr Alston? Perhaps we will never know.

Today the portrait hangs in the Macbeth Art Gallery in New York City where it is identified as the young Mrs. Alton.


## THE MACO LIGHT

At Maco in the flatlands of southeastern North Carolina Joe Baldwin is still carrying a lantern looking for his head since 1868 when he fell from a train and got his head cut off.

The ghost of Old Joe came back to try and get the body and head together. That's why you can see his lantern glowing along the tracks.

President Grover Cleveland reported he saw the light. Others including an investigator from Washington and many railroadmen who make the run past Maco also said they had seen it. They all agree it's Joe Baldwin's ghost looking for his head.

## MAGIC HOOFPRINTS

Around the town of Bath folks say the devil was riding a strange horse to run in a horse race one Sunday. Jesse Elliott was preparing his horse for a race. The stranger riding a black horse met Elliott. They talked awhile and Elliott challenged the stranger to a race.

Just as they started, Elliott's horse bolted and dug his hoofs into the earth and threw Elliott against a big tree, killing him instantly. The stranger disappeared and was never seen again.

The hoofprints are there today after more than 150 years. If grain is put in the tracks the birds will not eat it. Nobody can explain the holes — just the work of the devil. You can see them near Bath on the Camp Leech Road.

## THE DEVIL'S TRAMPING GROUND

Near the Uwharrie Mountains is a small circle where nothing will grow. Some of the people around this place say it is bare because Satan takes his nightly walks here. The people of Chatham County around Siler City call the strange spot "The Devil's Tramping Grounds".

Those who have visited the spot say you can lay a stick or a stone in the circle at evening and by morning there is nothing in the circle. Could it be that the devil kicks them away on his nightly walk?

Sometimes brave boys will camp near this place in hopes to see the devil. One story is told that a group of college students put their tent in the circle and went to sleep. These boys say that they have never recovered from the horror they experienced that night. To find this place take highway 902, a strip of pavement that links highways 421 and 22 between Siler City and Pinehurst. There is a marker designating the area as "The Devil's Tramping Ground."

## CONNESTEE

Near the town of Brevard is a beautiful waterfall called Connestee. This is a legend of the Cherokee Indians. We are told that many years ago a young Englishman was wounded and captured by the Cherokees. The Indians spared his life and he fell in love with Princess Connestee who nursed him back to health. The lovers often sat by the waterfall. The Indian Chief Wahlla gave his consent to their marriage. After they were married one day at the trading post getting supplies, her husband was persuaded by his friends to return to his own people. When he told her he was leaving to go back to his people this was too much for the heartbroken Indian wife. She did not wish to live so she threw herself over the falls and was killed. It is said that sometimes you may see her tragic figure in the gorge below.

## JUDACULLA

This is another Cherokee Indian legend. You remember the stories of Paul Bunyan who was the giant of the northwest woods. Judaculla was the giant of the Cherokees. He was taller than the tallest trees. He could step from one mountain to another. When he spoke, the heavens rumbled and the creatures of the earth trembled at this giant. He was the god of the hunt.

## BROWN MOUNTAIN LIGHTS

The old natives of North Carolina believed the lights were the devils and they danced in the sky above Brown Mountain when the moon went to bed and the stars blinked sleepily. Nobody really knows how long these lights have been seen over the mountain. For more than a half century the scientists have been trying to reason why they are there.

Some of the natives think it is the reflection from the fires of the liquor stills in the mountains.

The best place to see the lights is from the Parkway through the Blue Ridge Mountains at Wiseman's View, a very dangerous ledge. The lights appear all through the year, but the fall seems the best time to see them. The lights pop up and shine for a few seconds, then rise rapidly in the air high above the mountain top, then as if unsure of the path they should take, they fade out quickly.

LISTEN TO THE RECORD "BROWN MOUNTAIN LIGHTS".

## WHERE THE SNOW FALLS UPSIDE DOWN

At Blowing Rock high in the Blue Ridge Mountains, the snow falls upside down. The Cherokees say two braves fought near the ledge of a cliff for the hand of the chieftain's daughter. One warrior was cast over the cliff. At once the maiden realized the defeated brave was the one she really loved and she pleaded to the God of The Winds to save him. The warrior was returned to her safely.

Still another Cherokee legend says that Wenonah, lovely daughter of Chieftain Osseo, rejected her lover, Kwasind, who in dejection cast himself over the cliff of Blowing Rock. Wenonah was very sorry and prayed to the Great Spirit and petitioned both the Great West Wind and the gentle South Wind to bring her lover back. Together they blew Kwasind back up the cliff and into Wenonah's outstretched arms and they lived happily ever after. And the winds have been blowing there at Blowing Rock ever after.

Blowing Rock remains the only place on earth where the "snow falls upside down."

*Blowing Rock*

There are other legends such as The Lost Colony, Nag's Head, Piney Prospect, Blackbeard and many more.

FIND OTHER LEGENDS AND TELL TO THE CLASS.

Remember that legends are stories of some wonderful event which cannot be proved. They are handed down from one generation to another. For centuries historians have been baffled by some of the legends. Then others have only been remembered in the localities where the events occurred.

# NORTH CAROLINA PIRATES

North Carolina for years had been the home of pirates. In early days they raided shipping along the rough coastal waters of Carolina. They liked smaller ships so that they could strike fast and get away to hide in a hurry. Two pirates stand out above all others: Edward Teach, better known as "Blackbeard", because he wore a long black beard. He would plait it into little pig tails tied with colored ribbons. Just before a battle he would place small candles in his beard and light them as he stormed a ship at night to make him look more hideous. He looked like a firecracker ready to explode. He had a belt filled with pistols and daggers. Across his chest were several pistols cocked ready to fire. He was more feared than the devil by the sailors. Blackbeard was killed in 1718 by Robert Maynard of the Royal British Navy. Maynard cut off Blackbeard's head and let it hang from the bow of the ship.

The other pirate was Stede Bonnet. He was captured and taken to Charleston to be hanged. No stone marks his grave. The sea waters have washed away all traces of his final resting place.

The women were not to be outdone, so they had two women pirates. They were Anne Bonney and Mary Read. They were fierce and courageous. Anne Bonney was captured, tried, and sentenced but was never hanged. Mary died of a fever in jail. It was never known whether the lady pirates collaborated with Blackbeard or not.

Flags on the pirates'ships played important roles. They were to strike terror into the hearts of their victims. Some were red. The most popular design was the skull and crossbones. Sometimes the entire skeleton was used. At a distance they would fly a friendly flag like the Union Jack.

Often if the pirates met strong resistance they would flee rather than fight. Then again they would take the passengers as prisoners and let them go when the ships had been robbed. Not many were made to "walk the plank".

BLACKBEARD is called North Carolina's own pirate. However, he was not a native. He was born in England. He was "the fiercest pirate of them all". He was a tall man. His bushy beard was pitch black, which gave him his name. The death of Blackbeard marked the end of the "Golden Age of Piracy" in North Carolina.

READ "The Pirates of Colonial North Carolina", by Hugh F. Rankin.

FIND out all you can about BLACKBEARD.

**Blackbeard**

# WHY WE ARE CALLED "TAR HEELS"

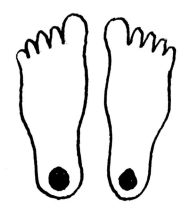

When North Carolinians get together for a good time, they love to sing:
"I'm a Tar Heel born,
I'm a Tar Heel bred,
And when I die,
I'm a Tar Heel dead."
The music and words authors are unknown, yet these words are a part of the song, "Hark the Sound of Tar Heel Voices", from the music of Amici.

There are many legends about how we got the name "Tar Heels". It started when North Carolina was a colony and still belonged to England. The coastal lands were covered with green pines and when they were cut, or notched, high upon the trunk, the thick, sticky liquid (raw turpentine) flowed slowly out into the can. It was boiled, made into rosin, tar and pitch. These products were used in shipbuilding to make the vessel waterproof. The tar was sent back to England where it brought a good price. The people of North Carolina had so much turpentine from the trees that the people were called "Tar Burners" or "Tar Boilers". The nickname was given to North Carolina as the *Turpentine State,* or the *Tar-Turpentine State.*

*A "Tar Heel"*
*sees*
*where tar comes*
*from —*
*raw turpentine.*

The poor North Carolina farmer worked with the hot turpentine and was barefoot. Therefore, the bottom of his feet had black tar on them. It was hard to get the tar off. People would say, "Look at that tar heel." A Confederate general admiring his troops fighting with such grim determination remarked, "That regiment of North Carolinians must have tar on their heels to make them stick as they do."

The favorite Governor Vance of North Carolina told the soldiers during the war how proud he was of his fellow "Tar Heels".

The nickname has stuck and every North Carolinian wants to be known as a true "TAR HEEL".

FIND OTHER STORIES ABOUT THE ORIGINATION OF "TAR HEELS".

# THE NORTH CAROLINA STATE FLAG

On May 20, 1861, our first state flag was adopted; but the one we fly today was adopted in 1885.

The flag is made up of three equal parts. The blue union which is perpendicular with the staff has a central white star bordered by N and C. Above in gold letters is May 20th, 1775, the date of the signing of the Mecklenburg Declaration of Independence. Below is April 12th, 1776, the date of the Halifax Resolves. The *waving* part of the flag consists of two equal horizontal parts with red on top and white on the bottom.

DRAW AND COLOR THE FLAG.

# THE GREAT SEAL

Examine the 2¼ inch seal shown below.

The figure to the left is LIBERTY, holding the Constitution in the right hand and in the left hand a pole with a cap. PLENTY is sitting down and holds three heads of wheat in her extended right hand. The Horn of Plenty on her left is running over. The Latin at the bottom, "Esse Quam Videri" means "To be rather than to seem".

What does the date "May 20, 1775" mean?

# THE SONG, "THE OLD NORTH STATE"

"The Old North State" became the official State Song in 1927. The author of the words of the song was Judge William Gaston. A group of Swiss Bell Ringers at a program given in Raleigh in 1835 sang a song that appealed to several North Carolina girls, who hummed it over and over on the way home. The next day two of them begged a copy of the music from the leader of the company and that night sang the melody under the window of Judge Gaston's house. He listened and said, "But there should be some words to such a pretty tune." He wrote the words to the tune. The first printing of the song is found in Wiley's North Carolina Reader, published in 1851. The Song was made the official State Song of North Carolina in 1927.

In the early days the song was a folk song that was sung orally from one generation to the next. It has been rearranged at different times for bands.

Let's sing this fine old song together.

READ: "Louisa and the State Song" — N. C. Parade by Richard Walser.

# THE STATE MOTTO

The State's motto appears on the Great Seal and the flag. It was adopted in 1893. The Latin, "Esse Quam Videri", is translated, "To Be Rather Than to Seem." It is found in Cicero's essay on Friendship where he wrote: "Virtute enum ipsa non multi praediti esse quam videri volunt", meaning "for indeed not so many wish to be endowed with virtue as to wish to seem to be."

By an act of the General Assembly of **1927,** the song known as "The Old North State" was legally adopted as the official song of the State of North Carolina.

# THE OLD NORTH STATE

*(Traditional air as sung in 1926)*

WILLIAM GASTON

Collected and arranged
by MRS. E. E. RANDOLPH

**With spirit**

1. Car - o - li - na! Car - o - li - na! heav-en's bless-ings at - tend her,
2. Tho' she en - vies not oth - ers, their mer - it - ed glo - ry,
3. Then let all those who love us, love the land that we live in,

While we live we will cher-ish, pro - tect and de - fend her, Tho' the
Say whose name stands the fore-most, in lib - er-ty's sto - ry, Tho' too
As hap - py a re - gion as on this side of heav - en, Where

scorn-er may sneer at and wit - lings de-fame her, Still our hearts swell with
true to her self e'er to crouch to op - pres-sion, Who can yield to just
plen - ty and peace, love and joy smile be - fore us, Raise a - loud, raise to -

CHORUS

glad-ness when ev - er we name her.
rule a more loy - al sub - mis - sion. Hur - rah! Hur - rah! the
geth - er the heart thrill-ing cho - rus.

*rit.*

Old North State for - ev - er, Hur - rah! Hur - rah! the good Old North State.

# THE STATE BIRD
# AND FLOWER

The cardinal is North Carolina's official bird adopted in 1943. The cardinal is also known as the redbird. It has brilliant crimson plumage. His song is very cheerful. If you have a good supply of sunflower seed he will stay close to your feeding station. The cardinal stays all year round in North Carolina.

The dogwood is the State Flower of North Carolina and was adopted in 1941.

FIND THE LEGEND OF THE DOGWOOD AND MAKE A REPORT.

# THE STATE TREE, STATE MAMMAL, STATE SHELL AND STATE INSECT

The pine tree was officially adopted as the STATE TREE in 1963.

There are 8 kinds of pine trees in North Carolina.

HOW MANY CAN YOU NAME?

In 1969 the gray squirrel was officially adopted as the STATE MAMMAL.

MAKE A REPORT ON THIS ANIMAL.

The General Assembly of 1965 designated the Scotch Bonnet as the STATE SHELL. This shell is light tan to white with rows of brown squares. It is very rare.

When you are at the beach look for a Scotch Bonnet Shell.

MAKE A REPORT ON THE HONEYBEE.

READ: The Beginning Knowledge Book of BEES AND WASPS by Jay Heavlin (Rutledge Books).

THE SCOTCH BONNET
SPIRES 'B
*(Phalium Granulatum)*

**The Honeybee**

# THE STATE FISH

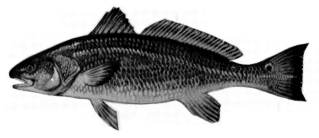

**CHANNEL BASS** *Sciaenops ocellata*
(Red drum, Puppy drum, Spot tail bass, Redfish)

(Courtesy, N.C. Dept. of Natural & Economic Resources)

# DO YOU KNOW THESE FACTS ABOUT NORTH CAROLINA?

The colors of the State are blue and red. They were adopted in 1945.

There are more than 70 lakes with recreational facilities in the State.

The nation's largest artillery post is Fort Bragg.

Washington, North Carolina, was the first town named for George Washington. (1775)

North Carolina did not vote for Washington as 1st President. Why? Neither did North Carolina vote for Jefferson Davis as President of the Confederacy. Why?

At the opening of the War Between the States every member of the senior class at the University of North Carolina enlisted.

The town of Murphy is closer to 6 other state capitals than to Raleigh. NAME THEM.

Manteo was the first American Indian to adopt the Christian religion.

Cabarrus County was named for Stephen Cabarrus, a Frenchman.

"Babe" Ruth (George Herman Ruth) hit his first home run in professional baseball in Fayetteville in 1914.

In 1875 in North Carolina the spectacle that drew the largest crowds were hangings, where up to 12,000 people attended.

The N.C. Mutual Life Insurance Co. of Durham is the largest business in the world owned and operated by blacks.

North Carolina was the first state in the whole United States to appropriate public tax money ($1,000,000) to buy art treasures for its State Museum.

At one time North Carolina had 100 covered bridges but now has only 3 left. WHERE ARE THEY?

# WHO WAS I?

1. I was the only North Carolinian who became the First Lady of the United States.
2. I was interested in education and tobacco and a large southern university bears my name.
3. I was a famous hunter. I left North Carolina and went to Kentucky.
4. I was a governor during the Civil War and a County was named after me.
5. I was an ambassador and wrote a biography of Woodrow Wilson.
6. I was the first State Superintendent of Education in North Carolina.
7. I was a governor and an educator and it was said that the last word I uttered before dying was "Education".
8. I was King George III's wife.
9. I was born near Pineville and I was 11th president of the U.S.
10. *We* were the first Indians to go to England.
11. I was a pirate and my real name was "Teach".
12. I attended Davidson College and later became President.

ANSWERS:

1. nosidam yellod
2. ekudbsemaj
3. enoobleinad
4. ecnavbnolubez
5. sleinadsuhpesoj
6. yeliwhnivlac
7. kcocyabselrahc
8. ettolrahcneeuq
9. klopxonksemaj
10. esehcnaw&oetnam
11. draebkcalb
12. nosliwwordoow

# NORTH CAROLINA

N   is for North Carolina.

O   is for Ocracoke on the Outerbanks.

R   is for Rutherfordton where Bechtler's gold coins were minted.

T   is for "Tar Heels".

H   is for Hatteras Lighthouse.


C   is for King Carolus and Carolina's name.

A   is for Asheville near the famous Biltmore House.

R   is for Raleigh, our State Capital.

O   is for "Old North State", our State Song.

L   is for "Lost Colony" at Roanoke Island.

I   is for Indians in North Carolina

N   is for Nag's Head.

A   is for Governor Aycock, the "Educational Governor".

# THE GOODLIEST LAND

T    is for THINKING about North Carolina.

H    is for HUNT for interesting stories about North Carolina.

E    is for one never sees ENOUGH of North Carolina.

G    is for GOD who made beautiful North Carolina.

O    is for OUGHT to see North Carolina *first*.

O    is for OBEY North Carolina traffic laws.

D    is for DO no harm to North Carolina beauty . . . DON'T be a litterbug!

L    is for LISTEN . . . you may hear the Cardinal sing.

I    is for INVITE your friends to visit North Carolina.

E    is for EAT a North Carolina apple a day to keep the doctor away.

S    is for SAFETY wherever you go in North Carolina.

T    is for TOO BAD if you don't practice SAFETY.

L    is for LIKING North Carolina so well that you take good care of her.

A    is for AREN'T you proud of North Carolina?

N    is for NOW remember how your ancestors worked to make North Carolina great.

D    is for DO your best to preserve forever our GOODLIEST LAND.

# "TOAST to the OLD NORTH STATE"

Here's to the land of the Long-Leaf Pine,
The Summer land where the sun doth shine;
Where the weak grow strong and the strong grow great;
Here's to "Down Home", the Old North State!

Here's to the land of cotton bloom white,
Where the scuppernong perfumes the breeze at night;
Where the soft southern moss and jessamine mate,
'Neath the murmuring pines of the Old North State!

Here's to the land where the galax grows,
Where the rhododendron's rosette glows;
Where soars Mount Mitchell's summit great,
In the "Land of the Sky," in the Old North State!

Here's to the land where maidens are fair,
Where friends are true, and cold hearts are rare;
The near land, the dear land whatever fate,
The blest land, the best land, the Old North State!

(On May 20, 1904 at a club meeting in Richmond, Va., Dr. J. Allison Hodges asked his visitor from Raleigh to give "a toast to the Old North State." Mrs. Leonora Martin picked up an old envelope and on it hastily wrote the toast. In 1932 Mrs. Mary Burke Kerr of Clinton wrote the music and dedicated the song to the school children of North Carolina. May 21, 1957 State Bill No. 305 established the toast. For details read Sturgis L. Hedrick's story in *The New East*.)

# ABOUT THE AUTHOR

Ozell Kiser Freeman was born in historic Kings Mountain, North Carolina. She attended the Plonk School of Creative Arts in Asheville and finished her education at Lenoir Rhyne College. She has taught in all of the elementary grades during her over thirty years of teaching in North Carolina, and has taught at Kings Mountain, Durham and Salisbury. She is a member of the Epsilon Chapter of the Delta Kappa Gamma Society, International; the National Education Association; the North Carolina Association of Educators; the Association of Childhood Educators; the North Carolina Association of Classroom Teachers; the North Carolina Society for the Preservation of Antiquities; the Historic Salisbury Foundation; Haven Lutheran Church and Auxiliaries, and the Salisbury Woman's Club. In 1974 she was "Teacher of the Year" for Salisbury City Schools and for NCAE District 5. In 1975 she won the Terry Sanford Award for the District. Lenoir-Rhyne College honored her with the 1975 Distinguished Alumnus Award.

She is the wife of Glenn David Freeman, President of Isenhour-Freeman Insurance & Realty Co., Inc. He is an alumnus of the University of North Carolina at Chapel Hill. Together they have toured all of North Carolina, much of the United States and many foreign countries.

# BIBLIOGRAPHY

Allen, W.C.—The Story of Our State—North Carolina

Brawley, James—History of Rowan County

Camp, Cordelia—The Influence of Geography Upon Early North Carolina

Carpenter, Allan—North Carolina From Its Glorious Past to the Present

Corey, Faris Jane—North Carolina Firsts

Cranford, Fred—The Waldenses of Burke County

Draper, Lyman C.—Kings Mountain and Its Heroes

Edmunds—Tar Heel Track the Century

Goerch, Carl—Down Home

Griffin, Clarence W.—History of Old Tryon and Rutherfordton

Hamlin, C.H.—Ninety Bits of North Carolina Biography

Hammer, Jr. Carl—Rhinelanders on the Yadkin

Harden, John—The Devil's Tramping Ground and Other North Carolina Mystery Stories

Harlow—North Carolina History

Henderson, Archibald—The Old North State and the New

Henderson, Cornelia Wearn—Early Charlotte & Mecklenburg County

Henderson, Moffit Sinclair—A Long Long Day For November

Lee, E. Lawrence—Indian Wars of North Carolina 1663-1763

Lefler, Hugh Talmage—History of Colonial North Carolina

Lowery, John R.—Memoirs of a Country Doctor

McCorkle, Lutie Andrews—Old Time Stories of the Old North State

McNeer, May—The Story of the Southern Highlands

Meyer—The Highland Scots of North Carolina

Murphy, Archibald D.—North Carolina History, vol. I

Parker, Mattie Erma—Money Problems of Early Tar Heels

Parris, John—The Cherokee Story

Powell, William—North Carolina

Rankin—The Pirates of Colonial North Carolina

Roberts—All Illustrated Guide of Ghosts

Robinson, Blackwell P.—The Five Royal Governors of North Carolina

Rouse—North Carolina Picadillo

Rowe, Nellie M.—Discovering North Carolina

Rumple, Rev. Jethro—History of Rowan County

Sharpe, William—A New Geography of North Carolina vol. II, III and IV

Southern Living Magazine & The State Magazine

Spencer, Jr. Carl O.—Indian Lore

Underwood, Thomas—Cherokee Legends and the Trail of Tears

Van Noppen, Ina and John—Western North Carolina Since the Civil War

Weathers, Lee B.—Living Past of Cleveland County

Walser and Street—North Carolina Parade

Washburn, Benjamin Earle—A Country Doctor in the South Mountains

Whedbee, Charles Harry—Legends of the Outer Banks and Tar Heel Tidewater

Wheeler, John H.—Historical Sketches of North Carolina

Wigginton, Elliot—The Foxfire Book

Order pamphlets from Historical Publications Section, Division of Archives and History, 109 East Jones St., Raleigh, N.C. 27611:

"Guide to N.C. Historical Highway Markers"

"The North Carolina Historical Almanack"

"Indians in North Carolina"

"North Carolina During Reconstruction"

"North Carolina Governors 1585-1968"

"Dare County: A History"

Adolph L. Dial and David K. Eliades, Pembroke University Professors — "The Only Land I Know", A History of the Lumbee Indians

**WELCOME TO NORTH CAROLINA**

*They say, "A picture is worth a thousand words." On the pages that follow we hope that you will learn to love the OLD NORTH STATE more and more.*

**BLUEBIRD**

*The blue bird is becoming rare in North Carolina because he does not have a suitable home. BUILD A BLUEBIRD HOME and hang it about 8 ft. high. Snakes and cats are enemies.*

**TWEETSIE**

*Midway between Blowing Rock and Boone is "TWEETSIE", the 100 year old steam locomotive. The train ride with Indian attacks is thrilling.*

**ROAN MOUNTAIN**

*North Carolina and Tennessee meet near the top of ROAN MOUNTAIN, near Bakersville. The Rhododendron Festival held here annually in early June will give you a floral display you will never forget.*

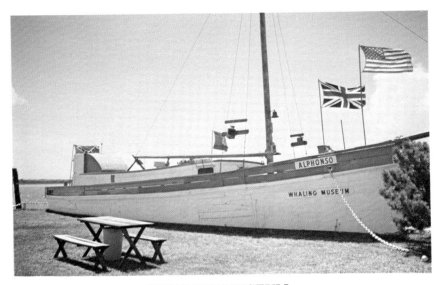

## WHALING MUSEUM

*The Whaling Museum at Beaufort reminds us that whale fishing was done in North Carolina in the 17th and 18th centuries. The whaling ship museum is on the site of the Spanish Invasion of 1747.*

## BEAUFORT

*The port town of Beaufort was founded in 1709. The town streets remain today as they were surveyed in 1713. The Col. Joseph Bell House was built in 1767 and has been restored. Hostess tours are provided.*

*In Beaufort there are over 120 homes and buildings over 100 years old.*

*Otway Burns is buried here UNDER A CANNON from his privateer "Snapdragon"*

**FIRST AIRPLANE**

*This full scale replica of the 1903 Wright Brothers' flying machine may be seen in the Memorial Building at Kill Devil Hills.*

**JOCKEY RIDGE**

*At Nag's Head is the highest sand dune in the United States . . . 138 ft. high. Others nearby exceed 100 ft. Sand skiing is a popular sport here.*

## SHORTIA GALACIFOLIA
### ("Oconee Bells")

*In 1788 Michaux, the French botanist, collected a specimen of this unknown plant "in the high country of Carolina" and carried it to Paris. Dr. Asa Gray of Harvard saw it there and named it "Shortia". For nearly 100 years no one could find this MYSTERY PLANT again. In McDowell County in 1877 G. M. Hyams, son of State Botanist M. E. Hyams, rediscovered the plant. Dr. Gray was notified and he announced it. (READ State Magazine: "Rarest Flower in N.C." Vol. 2, No. 39; and "Flower Lost for 100 Years". Vol. 27, No. 7.) Transylvania County and others now have Shortia. In March it has a pinkish-white flower.*

*Tobacco was grown by the Indians long before white men came to America. It became a major crop of the early colonists. North Carolina now grows more tobacco than any other state.* 137

## ORTON PLANTATION

*Now known for its beautiful gardens and grounds, it was a rice plantation in 1725. During the Civil War the Federal forces used Orton for a smallpox hospital. (Hwy. 133 south of Wilmington.)*

## TRYON PALACE GARDEN

*This beautiful formal garden of Tryon Palace at New Bern is typical of many old 18th century English gardens. Did you know that Mrs. James Edwin Latham gave this lovely garden to the state?*

## ST. THOMAS CHURCH

*St. Thomas Episcopal Church in Bath is the oldest standing church in North Carolina and is still being used. (Built 1734).*

## CHOWAN COUNTY COURT HOUSE

*The Chowan County Courthouse at Edenton was built in 1767. Offices of the Clerk of Court and the Register of Deeds have remained the same for over 200 years. The cupola was illuminated in 1789 when North Carolina ratified the U.S. Constitution. A banquet was held here for President Monroe in 1819.*

### EDENTON WATERFRONT

*The three cannons pointing toward Albemarle Sound were ordered in France by Benjamin Franklin in 1777. But when the colony could not pay with tobacco upon delivery on account of a bad crop, the ship's captain threw the cannons into the bay. They were later recovered and placed here. To the right is the Penelope Barker home which was moved here and now serves as Visitor Center. In 1774 it was Mrs. Barker who presided over the EDENTON TEA PARTY which met at the King house.*

### BRUNSWICK TOWN

*Old Brunswick, between Wilmington and Southport, was founded in 1726. It was occupied by the Spanish in 1748. Finally in 1775 the settlers deserted when the British came up the Cape Fear.*

## COVERED BRIDGE

*At one time North Carolina had over 100 covered bridges. Have you seen one? There are only three left. The Historical Society has restored the Bunker Hill Bridge east of Hickory on US 64 and 70. The Skeen Mill Bridge is 6 miles off US 64, 9 miles west of Asheboro. The Pisgah, pictured here, is off Hwy. 220, 14 miles southwest of Asheboro. It is 40 ft. long and cost $40 to build in 1920. What can you do to help preserve old historical treasures?*

## OUR THREE U.S. PRESIDENTS

*On State Capitol Square is this bronze monument to James Knox Polk, Andrew Jackson and Andrew Johnson.*

*In our great land of opportunity one of the boys here could be PRESIDENT some day. Or, YOU could be PRESIDENT.*

141

## HOME OF ZEBULON B. VANCE

*On May 13, 1830, Zeb Vance was born here. When he was 24, he was elected to the State House. Three years later he was elected U.S. Congressman. He became a colonel in the Civil War. He served three terms as Governor. He was elected four times to the U.S. Senate, where he died in office.*

*A prior resident of this home was Dr. Robert B. Vance, an uncle of Zeb Vance, who was a Congressman. In anger he made the mistake of challenging Samuel Price Carson to a duel over a political argument. Carson shot and killed him. (READ:* A Long, Long Day for November *by Moffitt Sinclair Henderson).*

## HOME OF THOMAS WOLFE

*The "Old Kentucky Home" (or "Dixieland") at 48 Spruce St., Asheville, has been restored as a Memorial to Thomas Wolfe. It recreates the setting for his book, "Look Homeward, Angel."*

## OLD MARKET
### . . . Fayetteville

*Built in 1838 on the site of Convention Hall which was the Capitol of North Carolina from 1789 to 1793. The U.S. Constitution was ratified there in 1789. General LaFayette spoke there. The city was the first named for him.*

## COMMUNITY BUILDING

*From 1856 until 1912 this beautiful building in Salisbury was used as a court house. It has been restored and is used as county office building. The Evelyn Pence painting of Elizabeth Maxwell Steele is here.*

143

## DR. JOSEPHUS HALL HOUSE

*The Historic Salisbury Foundation has restored this home built in 1820. Dr. Hall was a Civil War surgeon. The house contains original furnishings. Festive occasions such as Christmas are celebrated with "open house".*

## OLD SALEM

*Old Salem was founded by Moravians in 1766. It has been restored. Here at the gas light is the Hatter's Shop. George Washington ate and slept at Salem Tavern. Visit here and see how life was 200 years ago.*

## CHIMNEY ROCK

*Advertised as "Nature's 75 Mile Vista Overlooking Cliffs, Mountains and Lake Lure", it may be reached by Hwy. 64-74 west of Rutherfordton. A road leads to the base of the Chimney.*

### BRITTAIN PRESBYTERIAN CHURCH

*The church was organized 1768. A frame church was built in 1852, and brick-veneered in 1940. The interesting old cemetery has memorials to soldiers of the Revolutionary War and the Civil War. (Highway 64, about 7 miles north of Rutherfordton)*

## ROADS IN NORTH CAROLINA

*This South Toe River picture shows 3 ways of travel in early days. At first settlers used boats on the deeper streams. Later roads were made on the flat land beside the streams. Finally the railroads laid their cross ties and rails along the streams and valleys.*

*In the early days yokes of oxen as well as horses were used to pull wagons and sleds. In winter many roads were muddy and almost impassable. The ox was also used to plow the fields. In fact, it has been said that an ACRE was the amount of land a man could plow with an ox from dawn to dusk.*

146

### GRAVEL ROADS

*A few parts of North Carolina still have unpaved roads. But these roads are all-weather, since the school bus must travel there.*

### ROAD—BRIDGE

*This highway looks as if it is going to sea. Modern highways cross bodies of water where only ferries used to go. With over 174,000 miles of roads North Carolina has the largest State Highway system in the U.S.*

**GHOST TOWN . . . MAGGIE VALLEY**

*By cable car or steep road one can reach this old "western town" on the mountain. The stage coach is similar to the ones used on early roads in North Carolina.*

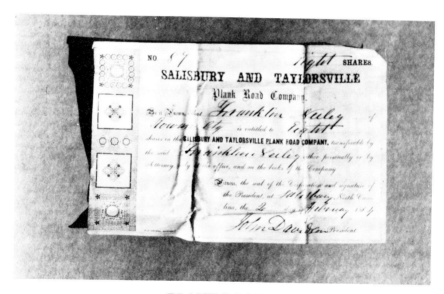

**PLANK ROAD**

*Up to about 1850 roads were few. Most roads were wagon wheel deep in mud in winter. In 1851 the Salisbury and Taylorsville Plank Road Company was chartered. This is a copy of one stock certificate signed by John Davidson, Pres. (Courtesy J. G. Hudson, Jr.). The plank road cost about $2,000 per mile to build. The road was completed from Salisbury to the Iredell County Line but no farther. Money gave out.*

148

## CHINQUA—PENN

*In 1959 Mrs. Jefferson Penn gave the 900 acre Chinqua-Penn Estate near Reidsville to the University of North Carolina. State UNC uses most of the land for farming and research. Greensboro UNC has opened the unique 27 room native stone and oak log mansion to the public. Treasures from all over the world (even from King Tut's Tomb) fill the "Y" shaped home. As the guide takes you from room to room it is like going from country to country . . . each different. (READ: Mrs. Margaret McConnell Holt's "Chinqua-Penn Plantation".)*

## GADDY'S GOOSE REFUGE

*Wild Canadian geese by the thousands once returned to Gaddy's Refuge year after year. The Gaddy's friendship and bushels of corn made these wild geese tame. Near Ansonville, but not now open to the public.*

149

## GRANDFATHER MOUNTAIN

*This may be the* oldest *mountain in the world! The elevation is 5,938 feet, and there is a road to the top. Here Hugh Morton has made a home for "Mildred", the bear. The MILE HIGH Swinging bridge is "cool".*

## PILOT MOUNTAIN

*Just over 20 miles northwest of Winston-Salem off Highway 52, Pilot Mountain juts 1500 feet above the surrounding countryside. Indians called it Jomeokee ("The Great Guide") since hunters could see it for miles and miles. Thousands and thousands of years ago surrounding country* may have been *level with the top of the mountain. Softer ground washed away leaving this durable rocky mountain standing up like a sore thumb by itself. Drive to the parking area and enjoy seeing far in each direction.*

## JONATHAN SEAGULL

*The Wright Brothers could have learned a lot from this graceful flying gull. He flies and flies on and on and never seems to get tired. Maybe it is because he sees so much beauty on the North Carolina Coast!*

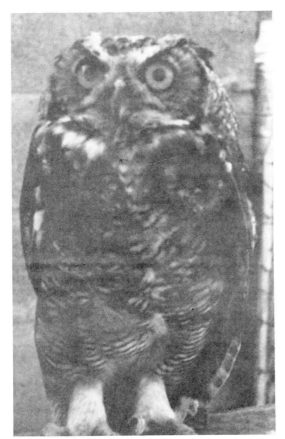

## THE WISE OLD OWL

*The Wise Old Owl surely does "GIVE A HOOT"! And so should we, and* not litter *this beautiful state of ours.*

151

## DEEP SEA FISHING

*Fishing boats go out to the inky-blue waters of the Gulf Stream just off the coast of North Carolina and catch some mighty big fish.*

*THE CHANNEL BASS WAS ADOPTED AS THE STATE SALT WATER FISH IN 1971. They usually weigh from 30 to 40 pounds but some have been caught up to 75 pounds.*

*Did the fisherman in the picture catch a Channel Bass?*

## THE USS NORTH CAROLINA

*This battle scarred ship of 40 months in the Pacific Ocean during World War II is majestic. She earned 12 battle stars. Open to the public 7 days a week, year around. During the summer "The Immortal Showboat" is shown each evening. Visit this beautiful battleship near Wilmington.*

## FARMING

Until about 1850 North Carolina was known as a state of "farmers". Cotton and tobacco were the big money crops. Farm exports to foreign markets are now over 400 million dollars. In 1969 there were 119,386 farms that produced and sold over one billion dollars worth of crops. The mule and the horse and plow have certainly given way to the tractor on North Carolina farms.

## TOBACCO AUCTION

Tobacco is a big money crop especially in eastern North Carolina. The auctioneer's chant as he sells the tobacco to the highest bidder is almost musical. Over half the value of agricultural and manufactured exports from North Carolina is tobacco.

**GREEN PASTURES**

North Carolina has many dairy farms. Fine beef cattle are raised. The lesson to be learned from this picture is that "grass is greener" in North Carolina. Young people don't have to go "over the fence" to other places for their best opportunities.

**SEA OATS**

North Carolina has many miles of beautiful sandy beaches. Sea Oats are often found on the mounds near the beaches.

## SLIDING ROCK FALLS

*Sliding down the slippery rock is fun in summer. A hand rail makes it easy to climb back for another slide. Off the Blue Ridge Parkway at Wagon Road Gap (Hwy. 276) go south toward the Cradle of Forestry in Pisgah National Forest. Bird Rock Falls is not far away. (Hwy. 110 exit south off Parkway). Also, Looking Glass Falls.*

## FISHING PIER

*North Carolina has one of the longest coast lines. Many fish have been caught from piers such as this . . . especially about sunrise.*

## EASTERN CONTINENTAL DIVIDE

*At this point the Eastern Continental Divide is 3322 feet above sea level. Rainfall to the west of this Divide flows into the Mississippi River. To the east it flows to the Atlantic Ocean. It is near the Blue Ridge Parkway.*

## MANUFACTURING

*Up to 1870 there was very little manufacturing in North Carolina. But the State woke up and is now in the top ten of manufacturing and agricultural exports. North Carolina leads the entire U.S. in the manufacture of textiles, tobacco, household furniture and brick. There are approximately 8,266 factories.*

*This photo shows Fiber Industries, Inc., near Salisbury, the world's largest polyester plant. In October, 1974, there were 2,785 employees.*

## CUPOLA HOUSE

*This unusual home restored in Edenton is the only surviving example in the South of this "Jetty" type. The second story over-hang was found in medieval Europe and 17th century New England. The period furnishings are very interesting.*

## MICHAEL BRAUN HOUSE

*Known as the "Old Stone House" near Granite Quarry, it was built in 1766. The walls are two feet thick. The foundation was 12 to 15 feet deep in the ground. It has been restored and is open to the public.*

## CONSTITUTION HOUSE . . . Halifax, N.C.

*The provincial Congress met in Halifax and appointed a committee to draw the first constitution for the State of North Carolina. In this house the men worked for 23 days and brought forth the Constitution on Dec. 6, 1776. VISIT HISTORIC HALIFAX where the "Halifax Resolves" were adopted in April 1776.*

## BATTLE OF GUILFORD COURTHOUSE . . . Mar. 15, 1781

*Lord Cornwallis' Redcoats "won" the battle over General Nathaniel Greene's men. But his loss of over 600 men so weakened Cornwallis that 7 months later he surrendered to Gen. Washington at Yorktown. VISIT THIS BATTLEFIELD.*

**JAMES KNOX POLK**
**1795-1849**

*Near Pineville in Mecklenburg County James K. Polk was born. The reconstructed 2 story log home measures 16 ft. by 32 ft. . . . 2 rooms down, 2 up. Heated by fireplace. Kitchen a separate building. VISIT THIS RESTORATION CENTER and see 30 minute film: "Who was Polk?"*

**HOUSE IN THE HORSESHOE**
**Built about 1772**

*Near Carthage on a horseshoe bend of the Deep River this plantation house of Col. Philip Alston has many bullet holes. In 1781 a Tory-Whig 2 hour skirmish took place. Tories tried to burn the house by sending a burning wagon load of straw against it. Alston had his wife wave the white flag. No wonder the children were hidden in the chimney.*

159

**SOMERSET PLACE**
**In Pettigrew State Park overlooking Lake Phelps.**

*About 1830 this 14 room plantation home built of heart cypress was the Collins Plantation. Slaves had dug a 6 mile canal 20 ft. wide for transportation and drainage of the swamps. Rice and corn were grown on about 2,000 acres. The Plantation grew to 20 buildings plus slave quarters. OPEN TO THE PUBLIC.*

**CHARLES BRANTLEY AYCOCK**

*Born Nov. 1, 1859 in this very plain small home . . . near Fremont. A typical 1870 one-room school building is in the Center with other old buildings. Aycock, the "Educational Governor" (1901-05) died in Alabama in 1912 while making a speech. He died with the word "education" on his lips.*

**HARPER HOUSE**
**At BATTLE OF BENTONVILLE, March 19-21, 1865.**

*The largest land battle ever fought in North Carolina raged here. Over 4,000 men fell. Gen. Joseph E. Johnston's 20,000 weary soldiers tried to stop Gen. Sherman's 60,000 troops, but failed. Sherman proceeded to Goldsboro. Johnston slipped away. The home of John and Amy Harper and their eight children was taken over for a hospital and stands today. VISIT THE CENTER AND BATTLEFIELD near Newton Grove & Hwy. 701.*

**BENNETT HOUSE**
**near Durham**

*April 12, 1865, Gen. Joseph E. Johnston met Gen. Sherman here and surrendered nearly 90,000 Confederate soldiers and their arms. The surrender saved North Carolina further havoc of war. General Lee had already surrendered at Appomattox Court House.*

*Mountain home with "suspended flue".*

## THE END

*As shown by the ducks in Gaddy's Lake,* this is the end. *But if the purpose of this book has inspired you, it will be the BEGINNING of a continuous and growing appreciation for the TAR HEEL STATE.*

# How The Good Lord Made The Old North State

HEARKEN, my friends, while I relate
How the Good Lord made the Old North State:
'Twas Saturday eve and the world was done
And the stars were made, and the moon and the sun,
And the Lord had finished Paradise
And had left over a great big slice,
So He took this slice of choicest earth
And North Carolina had her birth.

BENEATH the rays of the setting sun,
Silver He poured where the rivers run
And woods He made of gold and green,
With fruitful fields set in between,
And crystal lakes and purple hills
And purling brooks and rippling rills,
And then He took His finest dyes
And painted our opalescent skies.

THEN over this sister of Paradise
He scattered birds and butterflies
And myriads of flowers of heavenly hues
And wet them with celestial dews;
And then He said: "This land is blest,"
And the next day was His day of rest.
So this is how God made the great,
Progressive, glorious Old North State.

—Riley Scott.

# BATTLES OF REVOLUTION FOUGHT IN NORTH CAROLINA

Moore's Creek Bridge . . . . . . . . . . Feb. 27, 1776

Ramsour's Mill . . . . . . . . . . . . . June 20, 1780

Pacolet River . . . . . . . . . . . . . . July 14, 1780

Earles Ford . . . . . . . . . . . . . . . July 18, 1780

Cane Creek . . . . . . . . . . . . . . . Sept. 12, 1780

Wahab's Plantation . . . . . . . . . . . Sept. 21, 1780

Charlotte . . . . . . . . . . . . . . . . Sept. 26, 1780

Wilmington . . . . . . . . . . . . . . . Feb. 1, 1781

Cowan's Ford . . . . . . . . . . . . . . Feb. 1, 1781

Torrence Tavern . . . . . . . . . . . . . Feb. 1, 1781

Shallow Ford . . . . . . . . . . . . . . Feb. 6, 1781

Bruce's Cross Roads . . . . . . . . . . . Feb. 12, 1781

Haw River . . . . . . . . . . . . . . . . Feb. 25, 1781

Clapp's Mill . . . . . . . . . . . . . . . Mar. 2, 1781

Whitsell's Mill . . . . . . . . . . . . . . Mar. 6, 1781

Guilford Court House . . . . . . . . . . Mar. 15, 1781

Hillsboro . . . . . . . . . . . . . . . . Apr. 25, 1781

Hillsboro . . . . . . . . . . . . . . . . Sept. 13, 1781

Sudleys Mill (Cane Creek) . . . . . . . Sept. 13, 1781

(From The North Carolina Booklet, by Thomas M. Pittman, June 24, 1901)

# INDEX

# INDEX

## to Photographs of North Carolina, Pages 132-162

*NEW RIVER is the oldest river in the Western Hemisphere. Over 26 miles of its rapids and scenic gorges have been brought into the Federal Wild and Scenic River System. (Near West Jefferson.)*

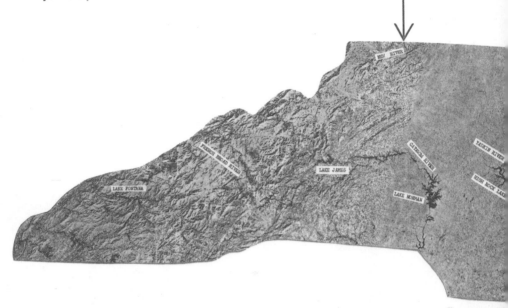

## OUTER SPACE PHOTO OF NORTH CAROLINA WITH BOUNDARIES AND IDENTIFICATIONS BY GLENN D. FREEMAN